M.

THE ROMANCE OF REDEMPTION

Studies in the Book of Ruth

M. R. De Haan

kregel
PUBLICATIONS

Grand Rapids, MI 49501

The Romance of Redemption by M. R. De Haan © 1996 by the M. R. De Haan Trust and published by Kregel Publications, P.O. Box 2607, Grand Rapids, Michigan 49501. All rights reserved.

Cover photo: Copyright © 1995 Kregel, Inc.
Cover design: Art Jacobs

3 4 5 6 printing/year 05 04

Printed in the United States of America

THE ROMANCE OF REDEMPTION

Studies in the Book of Ruth

Mr. Lawrence Thompson
PO Box 8798
Erie, PA 16505

Books by M. R. De Haan

Adventures in Faith
Bread for Each Day
Broken Things
The Chemistry of the Blood
Coming Events in Prophecy
Daniel the Prophet
The Days of Noah
Dear Doctor: I Have a Problem
508 Answers to Bible Questions
Genesis and Evolution
Studies in Hebrews
The Jew and Palestine in Prophecy
Studies in Jonah
Law or Grace
Our Daily Bread
Pentecost and After
Portraits of Christ in Genesis
Studies in Revelation
The Romance of Redemption
The Second Coming of Jesus
Signs of the Times
Simon Peter
Studies in First Corinthians
Studies in Galatians
The Tabernacle

Dedication

To our first-born daughter,

Ruth (De Haan) Haaksma,

who has brought us untold joy as
an obedient child, faithful wife,
and godly mother to her family,
this volume is gratefully dedicated.

Contents

Introduction

MANY excellent works have been written on the Book of Ruth, and in preparing this volume we are not impelled by a simple urge to write just "another book" on this subject. The Book of Ruth is, of course, inexhaustible as are all the inspired books of the Bible, but we have felt that one certain area of revelation has been relatively neglected. Most of the excellent works on Ruth have emphasized the truth of Redemption, and the Kinsman-Redeemer, and justly so. However, the prophetic significance of the story of Naomi and Ruth has not on the whole been treated with the thoroughness we feel it deserves. This can in part be explained by the fact that many events have transpired since these volumes were written, events which have cast a clearer light on the prophetic program of the Bible.

The recent return of Israel politically as a nation to the land of Palestine, and the conflict with the Arabs has illumined the story of Ruth with a significance but dimly seen before. In this volume, therefore, we have given special attention to the prophetic teaching of Ruth. If the emphasis on the prophetic aspect seems out of balance with the redemptive aspect so evident in Ruth, it is because there has been a lack of balance in the opposite direction, and because the prophetic picture in Ruth has been brought so prominently into focus in the current events of the past few years, both as regards Israel and the Church.

While Ruth is not called a "type" of the Church in the theological sense, nor is Naomi said to be a "type" of Israel, the narrative itself leaves no doubt that it is one of the most clear and detailed pictures of the dispensational dealings of God with both Israel and the Church as the Bride of Christ. The sojourn of the family of Naomi in the "land," their dispersion by famine, their sojourn in Gentile Moab, their sufferings and trials, follows the exact pattern of God's prophecies concerning Israel among the nations. The return of Naomi at the "good news" of restored fertility in the land has been experienced by Israel within the past decade. As Naomi returned but did not yet receive her lost inheritance until after the harvest, so Israel is back in the land, but still is dispossessed of most of her lost inheritance.

In the same way Ruth prefigures the Church of Christ. A Gentile, under the curse, estranged from God, she is brought in through the "exile" of Naomi. She believes in Naomi's God, and after resting at Boaz's feet during the dark night of threshing, she becomes the Bride of Boaz, the kinsman-redeemer, while Naomi's lost property is restored to her. It is a picture of the end of the age, Israel back in the land, the Church gleaning at the end of the harvest of this age, to be safely sheltered at the feet of her Boaz during the dark night of this earth's threshing time, the tribulation, to become the Bride of Christ, after the dark night is over and Israel will again possess the land in blessing.

This in brief is the prophetic picture of the events related in the Book of Ruth. We can only pray that the reader may receive as much blessing by the renewed study of the wonderful Book of Ruth as we ourselves have experienced in the preparation of this volume.

We are standing prophetically where Ruth and Naomi stood upon their arrival at Bethlehem from the land of Moab. Israel is back home, but still not in possession of her lost estate, which is in the hands of others. Ruth is gleaning in the fields gathering the last few ears. Soon the night of tribulation will settle, but not until after the rapture, and the Church is safely resting at the feet of Her Lord. In all of this the words of our Lord come with new meaning and emphasis as He declares in His last promise to us in the Scriptures:

He which testifieth these things saith, Surely I come quickly. Amen. Even so, come, Lord Jesus.

The grace of our Lord Jesus Christ be with you all. Amen. Revelation 22:20,21

—M. R. DeHaan

Grand Rapids, Michigan

Explanation

THE messages contained in this volume were originally prepared for broadcasting and were delivered over the two networks of the Mutual Broadcasting System and the American Broadcasting Company. They are reproduced almost exactly as they were delivered over the air, and with a minimum of revision and editing. As a result there is frequent repetition of the main theme — the prophetic picture of God's dispensational dealing with Israel and the Church. The repetitions are deliberate and planned for the purpose of emphasizing this much overlooked aspect of the Book of Ruth.

If after reading this volume you are inclined to object to the emphasis placed on the parallel between Naomi's experience and the history of Israel, we give as our reasons the following:

(1) The importance of the subject.

(2) The unmistakable analogy between the experience of Naomi and the history of Israel.

If the question is asked, "What authority have you for making Naomi's experience a picture of the prophetic program for Israel?", we answer, "It fits perfectly." We are reminded of Dr. Harry Ironside's answer to a similar question. He said, "If I have a lock and a large bunch of keys, how will I know which key belongs with the lock? The one which fits the lock is the right key." The history of Israel fits perfectly the story of Ruth.

CHAPTER ONE

A Family of Displaced Persons

IN presenting this series of expository studies on the Book of Ruth, we pray that we may be able, by the aid of the Holy Spirit, to impart some of the blessing to you, which we ourselves have received in the preparation of these messages, extending over a period of many months. Again and again we have been thrilled to the depths of our soul, as we discovered priceless jewels of the revelation of Christ in this wonderful book of redemption. Again and again we have been compelled to stop in our writing, overwhelmed with the richness of the teaching of this precious little volume of only four brief chapters. I trust you too will be stirred and thrilled and encouraged as we study together the touching love story of Boaz and Ruth. I would, therefore, before reading this volume, urge upon each of you, to read once again the entire Book of Ruth. It has only four short chapters. You can read it in less than twenty minutes. And then daily, for the next week, read it at least once. This little exercise will be of the greatest help to you in appreciating and understanding the messages in this book. A thorough knowledge of the contents of this little book will pay rich dividends in your study of the romance of Boaz and Ruth, and it will take you only twenty minutes a day.

A Story of Love

The Book of Ruth is a love story, relating the romance of a poor, widowed, Gentile servant girl, and a rich, powerful Jew of Bethlehem. The poor widow's name is Ruth; the wealthy Jew is Boaz. The story is full of pathos and drama, alternating sorrow and joy, tears and laughter, weeping and singing, and ends in typical storybook fashion with the marriage of the two lovers, and "they lived happily forever after." It reads like a novel, but it is not fiction, but a real story of love, between Ruth of Moab and Boaz of Bethlehem. It is one of the most clear and precious portraits and types of the love of our Redeemer, the Lord Jesus, for His bride, the Church.

Three Approaches

There are three definite lines of teaching in the Book of Ruth to which, by way of introduction, we would call your careful attention. As we have often mentioned, there are three approaches to the study of the Bible. Every Scripture has:

1. One primary, basic interpretation.
2. Many practical applications.
3. A prophetic revelation.

All three of these must be considered in studying the Word, to avoid being unbalanced and top-heavy in our Bible study. If we look only for the primary, doctrinal interpretation, we will be coldly correct and orthodox, but with no practical benefit. If on the other hand we look only for the practical applications, ignoring the primary interpretation, we may become warm and emotional, but drift into doctrinal error and fanaticism. And if we look only for the prophetic interpretation in the Bible, we become eschatological cranks, impractical visionaries, subject to all sorts of extreme prophetic interpretations.

To be a well-balanced Christian, we must always keep these three things clearly in mind:

1. Look for the primary interpretation; then,
2. Make your practical applications; and then,
3. You can evaluate the prophetic revelation without going off the "deep end" on prophecy. Just an example or two before we apply these rules to the Book of Ruth. In Exodus 3 we have Moses at the Burning Bush. The primary interpretation is unmistakably evident. It is a picture of the nation of Israel burning in the fires of affliction in Egypt, but supernaturally preserved by God. The practical application is for God's people in all time. We too, as the people of Israel, are often passing through the fire, for Jesus said, "In this world ye shall have tribulation." But the Lord has promised that we like the Burning Bush shall not be consumed, for Jesus adds, "But be of good cheer. I have overcome the world." And then comes the prophetic revelation of the Burning Bush. It is a picture of Israel's entire future history among the nations, always burning but never consumed, ultimately to become the fruitful vine of the Lord.

THE DRY BONES

One more illustration from Ezekiel 37. The dry bones of Ezekiel in the valley of the nations are by primary interpretation the nation of Israel (Ezek. 37:11). By application it may be referred to the Church in desperate need of a spiritual revival. And then the prophetic revelation points to Israel's final restoration and revival at the second coming of their Messiah and King. Apply this rule of threefold approach to the Scriptures (whenever you study it) and see how it will transform Bible study from a dull, drab, uninteresting exercise into a thrilling, satisfying experience.

APPLIED TO RUTH

It is the all too common mistake in Bible study and preaching to limit it to its practical application only, resulting in a stereotyped homiletical discourse on moral and ethical instructions, with a firstly, secondly and thirdly, and an appropriate story at the end. Valuable as exhortation is, and needful as moral and ethical instructions are in our teaching, they cannot really feed the soul with "strong meat," unless based upon the Scripturally correct interpretation. Our lives cannot be right, if our doctrine is wrong. We trust we have not wearied you with these dry instructions on how to get the most out of your Bible study, but we felt it necessary to have these facts clearly in mind, if you are to get the most profit from our study of the Book of Ruth.

The Book of Ruth is a marvelous example of this rule of three-fold approach to the Bible. The book has a primary interpretation, wonderful practical applications, and a thrilling supernatural prophetic revelation. The primary interpretation of the Book of Ruth brings us face to face with the message of redemption. A poor, widowed Gentile, a stranger to the covenants of promise, is redeemed by the wealthy Boaz. Boaz is a picture of Christ our Kinsman-Redeemer. Ruth is the picture of the Bride of Christ, the Church, unworthy in herself, but redeemed through infinite grace. This is the primary interpretation, the heart of the message.

The practical applications in the Book of Ruth are legion. The care of God for His exiled people (represented by Naomi), the providence of God in leading His children to their Redeemer, as seen in Ruth's gleaning in the field of Boaz, the security of the believer in the night of tribulation is seen in Ruth's lying protected at Boaz' feet, covered by his mantle during the long night of winnowing and threshing. All these and countless others are precious, practical applications of this touching story.

But there is also a grand and glorious prophetic revelation in the Book of Ruth. It gives in type, the history of the nation of Israel, and her final restoration after years of exile among the Gentiles, her repossession of her land, and the blessing of the Gentiles as a result of Israel's rejection. We shall see how Naomi is a picture of the nation of Israel, driven from her land by famine into a strange country, her tribulation and sorrow while there, then her return to her homeland, and how, during her exile, a Gentile Bride is being prepared for her Kinsman-Redeemer Boaz. We shall spend some time on this prophetic aspect of the Book of Ruth, while not overlooking the primary interpretation or its many practical applications. It has been an amazing and disturbing discovery for me, to find, in reading dozens of expositions of the Book of Ruth by scores of authors, that almost everyone has overlooked or ignored the prophetic aspect of this book. Almost every author whom I have read was occupied with the primary interpretation of redemption, or the practical applications and exhortations, and placed great emphasis on the moral and ethical instructions suggested in the book, but the prophetic lessons in the book, so evident and prominent in this volume, have been inexcusably overlooked by many. Valuable and important as is the primary interpretation and its practical applications, they are incomplete until we see them in the light of their prophetic revelation.

EVIDENCE OF GRACE

In our coming messages we shall point out the marvelous picture of God's dispensational dealing with the nation of

Israel (as seen in Naomi's exile), the calling out of the Church (as seen in the person of Ruth), the coming great tribulation, and the final glorious redemption of creation at the coming of the Messiah, Christ. But before we close this introductory chapter, we want to emphasize the glorious message of God's grace. Ruth was a Gentile from the country of Moab. This would legally bar her from a place in Israel's inheritance. The law emphatically forbade the intermarriage of an Hebrew with a Gentile. The law was explicit and unmistakable in its language. In Deuteronomy 7 we read concerning the Gentile nations in Canaan:

> . . . thou shalt smite them, and utterly destroy them; thou shalt make no covenant with them, nor shew mercy unto them:
> Neither shalt thou make marriages with them; thy daughter thou shalt not give unto his son, nor his daughter shalt thou take unto thy son (Deut. 7:2, 3).

Ruth was a Gentile and thus barred from the covenant nation by the law. She was legally excluded. But in addition, she was a Moabite concerning whom the law says in Deuteronomy 23:3,

> An Ammonite or Moabite shall not enter into the congregation of the LORD . . .

The law shut Ruth out, but grace took her in. By her marriage to Boaz, the Hebrew kinsman-redeemer, she entered the favored family of Israel. All this is a picture of the grace of God in Jesus Christ, our Kinsman Boaz, who took us, who were condemned under the law, aliens and strangers to God, doomed to death and destruction, and made us, by His redeeming work, the sons of God and members of the first family of heaven. Paul tells us:

> For what the law could not do, in that it was weak through the flesh, God sending his own Son in the likeness of sinful flesh, and for sin, condemned sin in the flesh:
>
> That the righteousness of the law might be fulfilled in us, who walk not after the flesh, but after the Spirit (Rom. 8:3, 4).

Application to Us

We are anxious for you to see the picture of yourself in this beautiful story of Ruth. Ruth is a picture of the helpless, hopeless sinner, alienated from God, stranger to the covenants of promise, condemned by the law, and doomed to eternal darkness. But there is one who is able to redeem. Ruth laid herself down at the feet of Boaz, and he recognized her helpless estate and received her and redeemed her. If you, my friend, will come humbly to Jesus' blessed, pierced feet, He too will place the robe of His righteousness over you and receive you, for He has said:

> Him that cometh unto me I will in no wise cast out (John 6:37).

Cast yourself upon His grace. Make no other claim than His mercy and grace, and thou shalt be saved.

> Not the labor of my hands
> Can fulfill Thy law's demands;
> Could my zeal no respite know.
> Could my tears forever flow,
> These for sin could not atone;
> Thou must save, and Thou Alone.

CHAPTER TWO

Exiles from Bethlehem

> Now it came to pass in the days when the judges ruled, that there was a famine in the land. And a certain man of Bethlehem-judah went to sojourn in the country of Moab, he, and his wife, and his two sons.
>
> And the name of the man was Elimelech, and the name of his wife Naomi, and the name of his two sons Mahlon and Chilion, Ephrathites of Bethlehem-judah. And they came into the country of Moab, and continued there (Ruth 1:1,2).

THE Book of Ruth is one of only two books in the entire Bible which is named for a woman. The other book is the Book of Esther, another intriguing story of redemption and the record of God's great care for His people. There are many books in the Scriptures which bear the names of men, such as Joshua, Samuel, Isaiah, Jeremiah in the Old Testament; and in the New Testament, Matthew, Mark, Luke, John, Timothy, Titus and others. It is not merely coincidence that the two books bearing the names of women should record the history of God's people in exile, out of their land, but miraculously redeemed and saved by a God-appointed Saviour.

RUTH AND ESTHER

In the Book of Ruth it was Boaz who became the redeemer of both Naomi's inheritance and Ruth's widowhood. In the Book of Esther, Mordecai, her cousin, became God's instrument for the saving of his people from destruction. May we not infer from this fact the unique place God gives to "woman" in the plan of redemption? Under the law women were not counted in the genealogy of the families of Israel. Man as the head of the family and of the woman, was given the place of recognition. But under grace all this is different. It was against the law for a Hebrew to marry a Gentile, so when Boaz married Ruth, he was doing what the law had strictly forbidden. It was, therefore, an act of grace. What was impossible under the law becomes possible under grace; viz, the salvation and redemption of condemned sinners.

SAME WITH ESTHER

The same was true of Queen Esther. In Ruth, a wealthy Jew marries a poor Gentile; in Esther, a wealthy Gentile king marries a poor Jewess (a D. P. from a conquered nation). Both were forbidden by law but made possible by grace. Both Ruth and Esther emphasize, therefore, the story of God's grace in delivering the nation of Israel and receiving the Gentiles into the covenant of grace.

STORY OF LOVE

But the Book of Ruth is not only a story of God's grace, but one of the most complete pictures of God's love for unworthy sinners. Ruth was a Moabitess, outside the covenant nation of Israel, without any legal claim to the blessing; but by virtue of the love of Boaz, who was an unmistakable type of the Redeemer, the Lord Jesus Christ, Ruth was able to enter the family of God's people. In all this we see a picture of God's plan of redemption for us, as Paul, in writing to Gentile believers, says in Ephesians 2:11-13,

> Wherefore remember, that ye being in time past Gentiles in the flesh, who are called Uncircumcision by that which is called the Circumcision in the flesh made by hands;
>
> That at that time ye were without Christ, being aliens from the commonwealth of Israel, and strangers from the covenants of promise, having no hope, and without God in the world:
>
> But now in Christ Jesus ye who sometimes were far off are made nigh by the blood of Christ.
>
> Now therefore ye are no more strangers and foreigners, but fellow citizens with the saints, and of the household of God (Eph. 2:11-13, 19).

How wonderfully this is illustrated in Ruth of Moab, the stranger and foreigner entering the family of Israel because of the love of Boaz, her Redeemer! This is the message of the Book of Ruth, the story of the grace of God toward the nation of Israel, and the love of Christ for poor, lost sinners. The book opens rather abruptly:

> Now it came to pass in the days when the judges ruled, that there was a famine in the land. And a certain man of Bethlehem-judah went to sojourn in the country of Moab, he, and his wife, and his two sons (Ruth 1:1).

Nothing is said about this family until the time of the famine which drove them from their native land. How long they had lived in Bethlehem we do not know; whether they were wealthy or in moderate circumstances we are not told. Nowhere else in the entire Bible are the characters in this family ever mentioned. All we know about them is contained in the four chapters of this book.

BOOK OF REDEMPTION

The book has one outstanding message — REDEMPTION. First we have the redemption of a lost land and possessions, the lost estate of the widow Naomi. Second, we have the redemption of a servant girl; and third, the redemption of a widow, the Moabitess, Ruth. In practically all the commentaries and writings on this book, much attention is given to the redemption of Ruth as typifying our redemption through Jesus Christ. Very little attention is given to the redemption of Naomi's lost inheritance which had been forfeited while she was absent in the land of Gentile exile. We, therefore, shall pay the more attention to this aspect of the narrative.

In the balance of this message we will give you a bare outline of the book in its entirety, and then take it up in greater detail as we go on. In the land of Judah, in the town of Bethlehem, lived a happy, prosperous family of Hebrews; Naomi, her husband Elimelech, and their two sons, Mahlon and Chilion. How long they lived here we do not know. Then a mighty famine broke out in the land. The members of this happy family were driven out of their country and went to the strange Gentile land of Moab. Here calamity after calamity, tragedy upon tragedy befell them. First the husband, Elimelech, died. Shortly after, the two sons, Mahlon and Chilion had married the two Moabitish women, Orpah and Ruth. Then they too sickened and died and Naomi was left a widow in a strange land with two widowed daughters-in-law.

After about ten years Naomi received word that the famine in Judea was over, and cheered by the hope of returning to her native land, she set out for Bethlehem. And with her went the Gentile widow Ruth. When they arrived in their land they found that Naomi had forfeited her claim to her inheritance, and the land which had belonged to her was now in the hands of another. Unless it could be redeemed and bought back, she was doomed to die in poverty. And right here the hero of our story came in. Boaz, a relative of Naomi, offered to restore (to buy back) by redemption, the lost land of Naomi, and in addition offered to marry the widow Ruth to save her from poverty and slavery and disgrace. And so after the harvest was over, Boaz restored Naomi to her possession by paying the redemption price, and Ruth became the wife of the Redeemer. In storybook fashion, the narrative ends with every one living happily forever afterward.

DISPENSATIONAL PICTURE

The dispensational picture is unmistakable and in the light of the Scriptures, we see in it a prophetic picture of God's dispensational dealing with His people throughout the ages. Naomi is a picture of the nation of Israel, living happily in the land of Canaan given to her by covenant promise. She is fruitful and prosperous. But the judgment of God falls upon the happy family and Israel experiences a judgment of famine. She is driven out of the land into exile among the nations and for the past twenty-five hundred years has been scattered among the Gentiles. Here she suffers tragedy upon tragedy, sorrow upon sorrow and becomes greatly reduced in number.

ENTER THE CHURCH

But while Israel like Naomi is pining in her dispersion, and suffering untold misery, God is preparing from among those very nations among which she is dispersed, a Bride for Israel's Redeemer. During this age of Israel's wandering (typified by Naomi's exile to Moab), God is preparing a Bride, the Church (pictured by Ruth), and when Israel returns to her own land that event will be followed by the wedding of the Church to Israel's Messiah, the mightier than Boaz.

Israel has almost reached the end of her sojourn in the Moab of dispersion among the Gentiles. Good news is coming from their native land. The people are fast going back. But during Israel's absence from Palestine, she has lost possession of the land, and others have taken over. But it will yet be restored, for soon Israel's Messiah, like Boaz, will redeem the nation, restore to her the land and become the Husband of the Bride, the Church; and usher in the golden age of earth's greatest blessing when Israel shall be fully restored to her land, and the land fully restored to her. How near that day must be! We are historically standing today exactly where Naomi and Ruth stood prophetically, when after ten years of exile in Moab, they arrived in the land of Judea during the days of the harvest. The harvest is almost done. The Church Age is almost ended. Only the gleanings must be gathered in, and then after a brief night of earth's threshing and winnowing in the Tribulation, when the chaff will be separated from the wheat, Jesus will come with His Bride who had been resting at His feet during the night of the terrible threshing. Israel will be delivered and the golden millennium of the world's greatest blessing will be ushered in.

Israel, as pictured by Naomi, is already back in the land as a nation, but the land has not yet been restored to her. Today Israel is waiting for her Messiah King to restore to her the full possession of the promise land covenanted to Abraham, Isaac, Jacob and David. After centuries, while Palestine was being wasted and barren and in the grip of famine, the good news has now been heralded around the world wherever the Naomi's of Israel's nation were scattered, "There is bread in Bethlehem; the famine is ending, come home to your native land." The desert is beginning to blossom like the rose, the waters of the Jordan are restoring the barren wastes of Judea, and modern technological knowledge is making the holy land buzz with activity and promise of unprecedented prosperity. When news came to Naomi that there was bread in Bethlehem, she went back. And the recent good news of Palestine's recovery and the promise of restoration to her national homeland has caused Israel to return, and she is today back as a nation in the land. And hand-in-hand with Israel's return is the Bride, the Church, going to meet her Husband. The day is almost gone and the gleanings are almost gathered. Soon the night will fall and the threshing of the nations begin. But before that comes, the Church like Ruth will take her place in full safety and rest at the feet of her coming Lord Jesus, her Redeemer Boaz.

And then, after the night of the Tribulation, comes the morning with full redemption. Naomi receives again her lost estate, Ruth becomes the Bride of Boaz, and the honeymoon of one thousand blessed years begins. Surely with Israel back in the land, with the Church gleaning the last few ears, we may expect at any moment the shout:

> Come, my people, enter thou into thy chambers, and shut thy doors about thee: hide thyself as it were for a little moment, until the indignation be overpast (Isa. 26:20).

This in barest outline is the prophetic dispensational message of the Book of Ruth. In coming chapters we shall elaborate on this marvelous revelation which occupies such an important place in the Word of God.

CHAPTER THREE

The Wife of Jehovah

TUCKED away in the midst of the historical books of the Old Testament is one little book of four brief chapters called the Book of Ruth. It is a love story of exquisite beauty and tenderness, a story of a wealthy Jew and his love for a poor Gentile widow. The story is not only interesting in the extreme, but replete with prophetic truth and one of the most complete accounts of God's wonderful plan of redemption.

The story reads like a novel, but rather than fiction, it is an actual account of the experience of a Jewish family, dispossessed of their home and seeking a livelihood in a foreign country. The time of the narrative is in the days of the Judges, shortly after Israel had entered the land of Canaan after centuries of slavery in Egypt.

BETHLEHEM

The scene opens with the departure of a family of four from their native city.

> Now it came to pass in the days when the judges ruled, that there was a famine in the land. And a certain man of Bethlehem-judah went to sojourn in the country of Moab, he, and his wife, and his two sons (Ruth 1:1).

To understand the deeper teaching of the Book of Ruth we must first of all notice carefully the "time" of the story. The opening verse gives us the key to its prophetic meaning, for the experience of this Jewish family from Bethlehem is a

27

beautiful picture of the entire history of the Jewish nation during the long years of her wandering outside the native land of Canaan. The narrative pinpoints the date of the story. It was in the days when the Judges ruled. Israel was without a King. It was a time of confusion and terror in the land. The Bible itself describes those days in the last verse of the Book of Judges:

> In those days there was no king in Israel: every man did that which was right in his own eyes (Judges 21:25).

Remember, therefore, that it was at a time when Israel was without a king, and there was no representative organized government and no national organization or unity. It suggests that future time when the family of Israel would again be without a king and a kingdom. The Book of Ruth, therefore, is placed in the Bible directly after the Book of Judges, and before the Kingdom Books of First and Second Samuel, Kings, and Chronicles. It suggests the days of Israel's disorganization among the nations, before the setting up of the Kingdom.

THE GREAT FAMINE

The next point to notice is that at this time of disorganization, this Jewish family of four was driven from its native city into a Gentile land, because of a famine in Bethlehem. The family migrated to the land of Moab, and there met with sorrow after sorrow, disaster upon disaster.

Famines in the Bible are usually a visitation of God in judgment, or in testing His people. Because of Israel's sins God had promised judgment upon them. In Leviticus 26 Moses had prophesied:

> If ye walk in my statutes, and keep my commandments, and do them;
> Then will I give you rain in due season, and the land

shall yield her increase, and the trees of the field shall yield their fruit (Lev. 26:3, 4).

But if ye will not hearken unto me, and will not do all these commandments . . .

I will also do this unto you; I will even appoint over you terror, and consumption, and the burning ague, that shall consume the eyes, and cause sorrow of heart: and ye shall sow your seed in vain, for your enemies shall eat it (Lev. 26:14, 16).

Famine was God's judgment upon disobedience. After relating the reason why this family fled from their home in Bethlehem and went to Moab (because of the famine in the land), we are given the details of their disastrous sojourn in this strange land.

And the name of the man was Elimelech, and the name of his wife Naomi, and the name of his two sons Mahlon and Chilion, Ephrathites of Bethlehem-judah. And they came into the country of Moab, and continued there (Ruth 1:2).

Before taking up the picture of God's redemption of this dispossessed family we wish to remind you again of the wonderful dispensational and prophetic picture suggested by this story of this Hebrew family. We have already seen that it points to a time when Israel is without a king, and driven from their land and sojourning among the Gentiles. One cannot fail to see in all this the history of God's covenant nation Israel.

A Happy Family

The story begins with this little family in Palestine. They were in the promised land and lived in Bethlehem which, significantly, means "The House of Bread." The names of the four members of this family are significant. Elimelech means "God is my King." Naomi means "The Pleasant One." The names suggest happiness and joy and contentment. They lived in the country of Judah which means "Praise." What a beautiful picture of a blessed people whose God was King, whose name was "The Pleasant One," living in Bethlehem, "The House of Bread," in Judah, the land of "Praise." Surely we cannot fail to see the picture of Israel in her golden days under David and Solomon under the blessing of God.

THE EXILED FAMILY

And then a terrible calamity befell this family and the judgment of God seemed to pour suddenly upon the happy quartet of Bethlehemites. A mighty famine came into the House of Bread, and God drove them out of the promised land of Canaan into the land of the Gentiles. The record is brief but dramatic. After they had sojourned for a while in the land of Moab, strangers among a strange people, we read the sad account:

> And Elimelech Naomi's husband died; and she was left, and her two sons (Ruth 1:3).

Naomi who had been wed to Elimelech, which means "God is my King," finds herself a widow in a strange land with two sickly sons, Mahlon and Chilion. The name, Mahlon, means "the sickly one," and Chilion means "the pining one." Naomi, bereaved of her husband, is left with these two sickly, pining sons who some time after, married two young ladies of Moab.

> And they [Mahlon and Chilion] took them wives of the women of Moab; the name of the one was Orpah, and the name of the other Ruth: and they dwelled there about ten years.
> And Mahlon and Chilion died also both of them; and the

woman was left of her two sons and her husband (Ruth 1:4, 5).

ISRAEL'S WIDOWHOOD

In the Scriptures the nation of Israel during her days of blessing in the land is represented as the wife of Jehovah. The Scriptures speak clearly concerning this relationship of Israel as the wife of Jehovah their God. This, of course, is not to be confused with the Church as the Bride of Christ. Israel was the wife of Jehovah, disowned for a season, but finally to be restored. The Church is betrothed to the Lord Jesus as the future Bride of the son of God. Naomi was the wife of Elimelech. The name, Elimelech, means "God is my King." This was Naomi's husband, whom she lost when she went into exile. But Ruth is the future Bride of the kinsman of Elimelech, the mighty Boaz. Bear these facts in mind. Naomi (Israel) is married to Elimelech (Jehovah). But she loses him in the land of her exile. A few Scriptures will clarify this little-known aspect of God's relationship to Israel. Isaiah in speaking of Israel's future redemption in the land after centuries of wanderings among the nations, refers to this age of wandering as Israel's widowhood. Speaking to Israel, he says:

> Fear not; for thou shalt not be ashamed: neither be thou confounded; for thou shalt not be put to shame: for thou shalt forget the shame of thy youth, and shalt not remember the reproach of thy widowhood any more.
>
> For thy Maker is thine husband: the LORD of hosts is his name; and thy Redeemer the Holy One of Israel; The God of the whole earth shall he be called.
>
> For the LORD hath called thee as a woman forsaken and grieved in spirit, and a wife of youth, when thou wast refused, saith thy God.
>
> For a small moment have I forsaken thee; but with great mercies will I gather thee.

In a little wrath I hid my face from thee for a moment; but with everlasting kindness will I have mercy on thee, saith the LORD thy Redeemer.

For the mountains shall depart, and the hills be removed; but my kindness shall not depart from thee, neither shall the covenant of my peace be removed, saith the LORD that hath mercy on thee (Isa. 54:4-8, 10).

Here is God's prophetic picture of God's past, present and future dealing with Israel. She was the wife of Jehovah, disowned because of her sin, but ultimately to be restored because of God's everlasting covenant of grace with Abraham, Isaac and Jacob.

NAOMI AND ELIMELECH

Surely one cannot fail to see in the experience of Naomi and her exile in Moab a picture of the nation. Naomi lost her husband and sojourned as a widow forsaken in a strange land. How striking the record:

And Elimelech Naomi's husband died; and she was left, and her two sons (Ruth 1:3).

Naomi, whose name means the "pleasant one," is a widow.

THE WIDOW IN HOSEA

For an even fuller picture of Israel during her exile among the nations we turn to the prophecy of Hosea.

Say ye unto your brethren, Ammi [my people]; and to your sisters, Ruhamah [the pitied one].

Plead with your mother, plead: for she is not my wife, neither am I her husband: let her therefore put away her whoredoms out of her sight, and her adulteries from between her breasts . . .

For their mother hath played the harlot: she that conceived them hath done shamefully . . . (Hosea 2:1, 2, 5).

Idolatry is called in the Bible, spiritual fornication, and compared to the unfaithfulness of a wife to her husband.

Because of this sin the nation was forsaken and disowned, scattered abroad, dispersed among the nations until the days of her repentance.

In the first chapter of Hosea the prophet dramatizes this broken fellowship of Israel and her husband Jehovah. In this chapter (which we suggest you study carefully for yourself) the prophet is to take for a wife a harlot by the name of Gomer (Hosea 1:3). To this union a son was born called Jezreel, because God said:

> . . . for yet a little while, and I will avenge the blood of Jezreel . . . and will cause to cease the kingdom of the house of Israel (Hosea 1:4).
>
> And she conceived again, and bare a daughter. And God said unto him, Call her name Lo-ruhamah: for I will no more have mercy upon the house of Israel . . .
>
> Now when she had weaned Lo-ruhamah, she conceived, and bare a son.
>
> Then said God, Call his name Lo-ammi: for ye are not my people, and I will not be your God (Hosea 1:6, 8, 9).

The prophecy is clear. Hosea is acting out God's judgment upon Israel, and compares her to an unfaithful wife who bears three children. The first was called Jezreel, meaning "God will sow or scatter you abroad." The daughter's name was Lo-ruhamah meaning "God will not have pity," and the third child's name was Lo-ammi, meaning "Ye are not my people." It was God's judgment in scattering the house of Israel.

Once more Hosea is commanded to marry another wife. The strange story is in Hosea 3.

> Then said the LORD unto me, Go yet, love a woman beloved of her friend, yet an adulteress, according to the love of the LORD toward the children of Israel, who look to other gods, and love flagons of wine.
>
> So I bought her to me for fifteen pieces of silver, and for

an homer of barley, and an half homer of barley (Hosea 3:1, 2).

Here again Israel is presented as the wife of Jehovah, but unfaithful to him, and, therefore, He puts her away for a season. The exposition follows in Hosea 3:4,

> For the children of Israel shall abide many days without a king, and without a prince, and without a sacrifice, and without an image, and without an ephod, and without teraphim.

THE DISPERSION

History stands as a literal fulfillment of this prophecy. After centuries of blessing in the land, Israel was unfaithful to her Jehovah husband, and He turned His face against her, drove her out of the land, scattered her among the nations, without a king, a prince and without a sacrifice. Here she has been for centuries, as a forsaken widow.

But God's dealing was for a purpose. It was to correct her and receive her as from the dead, and so Hosea 3 closes with:

> Afterward shall the children of Israel return, and seek the LORD their God, and David their king; and shall fear the LORD and His goodness in the latter days (Hosea 3:5).

Then shall Israel the estranged wife of Jehovah return to her God, according to Hosea 2:14-16,

> Therefore, behold, I [Jehovah] will allure her [Israel], and bring her into the wilderness, and speak comfortably unto her.
> And I will give her her vineyards from thence, and the valley of Achor for a door of hope: and she shall sing there, as in the days of her youth, and as in the day when she came up out of the land of Egypt.
> And it shall be at that day, saith the LORD, that thou shalt call me Ishi *[My Husband]*; and shalt call me no more Baali *[My Lord]*.

THE SOON RETURN

As Naomi was thrust out of Bethlehem by God's judgment, so Israel was thrust out of the land for her sin. As Naomi lost her husband in a strange country, so Israel was estranged from her Jehovah husband. As Naomi suffered and pined away among the Gentiles, so too with God's people. But like Naomi, it was only for a time and ultimately she will return to her homeland and possessions to be God's people forevermore.

Thus we see in the experience of Naomi in the Book of Ruth a glorious prophecy of the nation of Israel. In coming chapters we shall study Naomi's tribulation, bereavement and sorrow in the land of her exile as a picture of Israel's sojourn out of her land and among the nations.

AN APPLICATION

Before closing we would like to make a personal, practical application. In spite of Israel's unfaithfulness, her Jehovah God did not cast them off, but remained faithful to His covenant of grace, and after correcting her, He restores her to all her former glory. So too God chastens His children for their sins, but does not cast them off, but stands ready to restore them again the moment they repent and turn to Him.

Are you being chastened of the Lord? Then it is because God loves you, and is preparing you for a blessing and glory which could only come by loving correction and cleansing.

> If we confess our sins, he is faithful and just to forgive us our sins, and to cleanse us from all unrighteousness (I John 1:9).

CHAPTER FOUR

Israel Among the Nations

> And Elimelech Naomi's husband died; and she was left, and her two sons.
>
> And they took them wives of the women of Moab: the name of the one was Orpah, and the name of the other Ruth: and they dwelled there about ten years.
>
> And Mahlon and Chilion died also both of them; and the woman was left of her two sons and her husband (Ruth 1:3-5).

THE Book of Ruth, in addition to being a beautiful love story of Boaz and Ruth, is also a book of prophecy, for it clearly depicts the plan and purpose of God for the nation of Israel and for the Church as the Bride of Christ. This becomes apparent as we closely compare the experience of the family of Naomi with the past history and future promises to Israel. Naomi is a picture of the nation of Israel dwelling happily at the first in the land of their fathers. Then came the judgment of God and drove them from their homeland into a Gentile country where she sojourned for ten long years.

PINING AMONG THE NATIONS

The story of Naomi's sojourn in the land is brief but inexhaustible in its teaching. When Naomi's family fled from Bethlehem (the house of bread) they went to Moab. Moab was a son of the backslidden Lot, nephew of Abraham. After Lot's deliverance from Sodom, his two daughters gave him wine and made him drunken, and while in this drunken state, Lot became the father of the two children by his own daughters. The one son of incest was called Moab and the other Ben-ammi. They became the ancestors of the Moabites and the Ammonites. They represent the world of sin and corruption, and thus are symbols of God's curse. To this land the family of Naomi goes and it is no wonder that the next thing we read is that "Elimelech died." Elimelech means "God is my king." Like Naomi, the nation of Israel is driven from the land and loses the fellowship of God her king. They are now "Lo-ammi" — not my people; and as we have seen, the nation is represented as a widow, the disowned wife of Jehovah. God is no longer her King.

THE TWO SONS DIE

But the death of Elimelech was only the beginning of Naomi's tragic suffering in Moab. The next thing we read is the death of Mahlon and Chilion, shortly after their marriage to the two Moabitish women, Orpah and Ruth. Tragedy after tragedy befell poor Naomi. Her sojourn in Moab was a time of death and funerals till the family of four is reduced to one. It could go no farther without wiping out the name of the family forever.

PICTURE OF THE NATION

One cannot fail to see in all this an unmistakable picture of the nation of Israel. They too went out of the land into the place of the curse and found it only a place of death. Disowned by God, the nation was reduced until they too were few in number. The very names of the two sons of Naomi are suggestive of her sojourn in the land of the Gentiles. The name, Mahlon, means the "sickly or consumptive one," and Chilion means "the pining one." It was the place of consumption, of sorrow, of pining away, and a place of graves among a strange people.

Such for centuries has been the condition of the nation among the nations of the world, a widow, desolate, hopeless, homesick for the home of her youth and her God. But all this has been minutely foretold in greatest detail as far back as the days of Moses. Before Israel had set a foot in the land of Canaan, God had foretold exactly what their entire future history would be. First He had prophesied their prosperous possession of the land. In Leviticus we read:

> If ye walk in my statutes, and keep my commandments, and do them;
>
> Then will I give you rain in due season, and the land shall yield her increase, and the trees of the field shall yield their fruit.
>
> And your threshing shall reach unto the vintage, and the vintage shall reach unto the sowing time: and ye shall eat your bread to the full, and dwell in your land safely.
>
> And I will give peace in the land, and ye shall lie down, and none shall make you afraid: and I will rid evil beasts out of the land, neither shall the sword go through your land.
>
> And ye shall chase your enemies, and they shall fall before you by the sword.
>
> And five of you shall chase an hundred, and an hundred of you shall put ten thousand to flight: and your enemies shall fall before you by the sword.
>
> For I will have respect unto you, and make you fruitful, and multiply you, and establish my covenant with you.
>
> And ye shall eat old store, and bring forth the old because of the new.
>
> And I will set my tabernacle among you: and my soul shall not abhor you.
>
> And I will walk among you, and will be your God, and ye shall be my people (Lev. 26:3-12).

ALL WAS FULFILLED

Comment on these verses is hardly necessary. The history of David's glorious reign of victory, and Solomon's reign of uprecedented peace and prosperity stand as irrefutable evidence of the truth of these prophetic words. All this is illustrated in the sojourn of the happy family of Elimelech, Naomi, Mahlon and Chilion in Bethlehem of Judea. It is indeed the House of Bread. But there were conditions attached to this blessing, and when Israel failed to meet these conditions God drove them out, and scattered them among the Gentiles, where, like the family of Naomi, they met with sorrow, persecution, sickness, trouble and death. But all this too had been prophesied. Again reading in Leviticus 26:

> But if ye will not hearken unto me, and will not do all these commandments . . .
> I will also do this unto you; I will even appoint over you terror, consumption, and the burning ague, that shall consume the eyes, and cause sorrow of heart: and ye shall sow your seed in vain, for your enemies shall eat it (Lev. 26:14, 16).
> And I will bring the land into desolation: and your enemies which dwell therein shall be astonished at it.
> And I will scatter you among the heathen [nations], and will draw out a sword after you: and your land shall be desolate, and your cities waste . . .
> And ye shall perish among the heathen [nations], and the land of your enemies shall eat you up.
> And they that are left of you shall pine away in their iniquity in your enemies' lands (Lev. 26:32, 33, 38, 39).

Again comment seems quite unnecessary for history stands as evidence that this has happened in every detail. In 70 A.D. the pagan Titus captured Juda, sacked the city of Jerusalem, and scattered its inhabitants to the four corners of the earth where all these things have been experienced by them. We might quote passage after passage from the books of Moses and all the prophets to show further how meticulously God foretold her whole history in advance.

But this wandering in exile is not to last forever. There is also a return to the land of "milk and honey" prophesied. Not only are the prophets clear in their unbroken testimony concerning Israel's ultimate return to her homeland (now in progress), but it is also wonderfully illustrated in the Book of Ruth. While it is a story of tragedy, sorrow and death and suffering, it ends in a complete restoration of joy and happiness. Naomi fled to Moab in the hope of finding relief from the famine, but instead finds in this strange land only a place of graves.

Bereft of her husband and two sons, this poor widow is left in a foreign land among strangers, with two daughters-in-law, also widows. This continued for about ten years and at the end of the ten years she returns to her homeland, sees her Gentile daughter-in-law happily married to the wealthy Jewish land owner, Boaz. Then they all lived happily ever after.

ABOUT TEN YEARS

Before continuing the wonderful prophetic picture, we must call your attention to the length of time Naomi was in exile. Our verse (Ruth 1:4) says it was *about* ten years. It does not say *ten* years or *nine* years, but "about" ten years. We may also render it *almost ten years*. It was evidently more than nine but less than ten. Believing as we do in the verbal inspiration of the Scriptures, there must be some reason for the expression, "about ten years." In Bible numerics each number has a constant meaning. One is the number of sovereignty; two the number of division; three — completeness: four — the earth number; five — grace; six — the number of man; seven — perfection; eight — a new beginning; nine — judgment; and ten — testimony.

JUDGMENT AND TESTIMONY

Since nine is the number of judgment and ten is the number of testimony, we have in the expression, "about ten years," the end of the period of judgment (9 years) and the resumption of Naomi's testimony to the faithfulness of God in returning her to her land (10 years). After returning to Bethlehem, Ruth becomes the Gentile bride of the wealthy Hebrew, Boaz. Naomi's lost property is restored to her; and the story ends with Boaz and Ruth happily married, and Naomi a happy, happy grandmother living at peace in Bethlehem. This, in brief, is the story of Ruth, and I trust you have seen the picture of the history of God's chosen family of Israel.

THE HISTORY OF ISRAEL

We repeat, the family of Elimelech and Naomi is a picture of the nation of Israel. God had planted them in the promised land according to an everlasting covenant with Abraham, Isaac and Jacob. It was indeed a "House of Bread," a land flowing with milk and honey. And then because of their disobedience and sin, God's judgment fell upon the nation. Its land became barren, the enemy came and scattered them among the Gentiles where they have found a place of sorrow, tears, agony, persecution and death.

But they were not to remain there, for after "about" ten years, the nine years of "judgment" passed, and Ruth, the Gentile bride, is married to the kinsman-redeemer as a picture of the wedding and the marriage of the Bride, the Church, to her Lord and Husband, Jesus Christ; and the nation of Israel, typified by Naomi, restored to the land, becomes the nation of blessing to all the world.

The story of Ruth is today dispensationally almost finished. The nation of Israel has been dispersed all these centuries among the Gentiles where Elimelech, Mahlon and Chilion have been buried. During their exile, their land, the land of Canaan, has lain waste and famine-ridden. But the days of exile are about over. Israel, like Naomi of old, is on the way back to her ancient land, and today already is represented by the State of Israel in Palestine. Soon the marriage of the Church, foreshadowed by Ruth, will take place when the Lord Jesus, the Bridegroom so beautifully foreshadowed by Boaz, will shout from the air, and we shall rise to meet Him. Then He will return to this earth and Israel shall be fully restored to her lost inheritance.

The tale is almost done. The next thing is the coming of the Lord, Israel as a political sovereign state is already in the land. The next event, we believe, will be the coming again of our Saviour. The harvest will soon be over. The gleaning time is here. In closing — one question: What will happen to you when Jesus calls *you*? Ruth had to make a decision, or be left behind, and you too must make your decision before it is too late.

CHAPTER FIVE

The Mystery of the Ages

THE Book of Ruth is more than a story of love. It is also a story of redemption. One aspect of the narrative, however, has been almost totally overlooked. That is the dispensational and prophetic aspect of the book, giving us in some detail the prophetic picture of Israel's experience throughout the ages. The family of Naomi is a picture of the family of Israel. They lived happily in the promised land until the judgment of God fell upon them and a famine drove them out into the land of the Gentiles. Here suffering, agony, sorrow, and death haunted them until finally they returned to their homeland to have their land returned to them by their redeemer; and Ruth, the Gentile bride, becomes the wife of the Jewish landlord, Boaz.

In all this we have a prophetic picture of the nation of Israel. That nation dwelt in a land of blessing called in the Bible a "land flowing with milk and honey." And then the judgment of God fell upon them. They were driven out among the Gentiles where death followed them all the way.

While the family of Naomi was in the land of exile, they were reduced in number, for her husband, Elimelech died, and then her two sons, Mahlon and Chilion also (Ruth 1:3 and 5). Only one out of four (25 per cent) survived. and Naomi was left forsaken. This is an unmistakably

43

striking picture of Israel. In Deuteronomy 28 Moses had prophesied:

> And ye [Israel] shall be left few in number, whereas ye were as the stars of heaven for multitude; because thou wouldest not obey the voice of the LORD thy God . . .
> And the LORD shall scatter thee among all people, from the one end of the earth even unto the other; and there thou shalt serve other gods, which neither thou nor thy fathers have known, even wood and stone.
> And among these nations shalt thou find no ease, neither shall the sole of thy foot have rest: but the LORD shall give thee there a trembling heart, and failing of eyes, and sorrow of mind.
> And thy life shall hang in doubt before thee; and thou shalt fear day and night, and shalt have none assurance of thy life:
> In the morning thou shalt say, Would God it were even! and at even thou shalt say, Would God it were morning! for the fear of thine heart wherewith thou shalt fear, and for the sight of thine eyes which thou shalt see (Deut. 28:62, 64-67).

These words were spoken, remember, before Israel had even seen the promised land, yet have been fulfilled to the very letter. The reduction in number due to the persecutions of their oppressors at one time resulted in less than one million of the people of Israel being left in the world. Today there are over 18 million, 10 per cent of which are already in Palestine.

Pictured In Ruth

All these prophecies so minutely fulfilled are beautifully portrayed in the Book of Ruth. Naomi's family too was reduced to one-fourth its original number. In Moab she too found no ease and found no rest until she could return to her homeland. But in the providence of God, Naomi was sent to Moab to accomplish a great purpose in the plan of God. In Moab lived Ruth, the future bride of Naomi's kinsman, the mighty Boaz. To bring Ruth to Boaz, Naomi must be exiled to Moab. In this way God was able to bring to Boaz (type of the Lord Jesus) his bride, Ruth (type of the Church). To accomplish this, Naomi must be exiled from her land. And then after a bride for Boaz has been prepared, God brings Naomi back to her land and her inheritance.

THE MYSTERY OF THIS AGE

That this is a picture of God's dispensational plan is made clear in the Scriptures. Paul tells us that God set aside the nation of Israel out of her land in order that during her rejection He might call out the Bride of Christ, the Church, and then after that restore Israel again. Israel (represented by the family of Naomi) is in exile, but the Bride is almost ready, and Israel's deliverance is at hand.

Paul tells us of this deep mystery in Romans 11, speaking of the fact that Israel was set aside while the Church was called out:

> For I would not, brethren, that ye should be ignorant of this mystery, lest ye should be wise in your own conceits; that blindness in part is happened to Israel, UNTIL the fulness of the Gentiles be come in.
> And so all Israel shall be saved: as it is written . . . (Rom. 11:25, 26).

ALL THIS PROPHESIED

Israel's exile is temporary. It is only *until* the fullness of the Gentiles (the Church) be brought in. Just as Naomi returned to Bethlehem when Ruth was ready to go, so too one of these days the number of the redeemed will be full, and God will again visit His people.

Moses, who foretold Israel's dispersion and suffering in exile, also foretold their deliverance and return to the land. In Leviticus 26 we read:

> Then will I remember my covenant with Jacob . . . Isaac, . . . Abraham . . . and I will remember the land.
> . . . I will not cast them away . . . to destroy them utterly, and to break my covenant with them (Lev. 26:42, 44).

We quote again from Ezekiel 36:

> For I will take you from among the heathen [Gentiles], and gather you out of all countries, and will bring you into your *own land.*
> And ye shall dwell in the land that I gave to your fathers; and ye shall be my people, and I will be your God (Ezek. 36:24, 28).

And in Ezekiel 37:25 the prophet declares concerning Israel:

> And they shall dwell in the land that I have given unto Jacob my servant, wherein your fathers have dwelt; and they shall dwell therein, even they, and their children, and their children's children for ever. . . .

How near that time must be when we realize that already there is a company of the family of Israel in the land today known as the State of Israel.

GOOD NEWS FROM HOME

We return now to the narrative in Ruth and the return of Naomi to the land of her fathers after almost ten years of exile.

> Then she arose with her daughters in law, that she might return from the country of Moab: for she had heard in the country of Moab how that the Lord had visited his people in giving them bread.
> Wherefore she went forth out of the place where she was, and her two daughters in law with her; and they went on the way to return unto the land of Judah (Ruth 1:6, 7).

After nine long years in Moab, Naomi hears rumors of good news from Bethlehem and Judah. The land which had been gripped in famine, again has bread. The fields which were dry and parched are again green and verdant, and the desert places are beginning to blossom as the rose. Cheered by the good news from home, Naomi responds to her nostalgic longing for the land of her fathers and begins the trek back home.

But she is not to return alone, for Ruth, the widow, is to go with her and become the bride of Naomi's redeemer, Boaz. All this is intensely interesting in the light of God's dealing with His people. Naomi is an unmistakable picture of Israel driven out into dispersion, while the bride of the Redeemer (Ruth) is being prepared for her husband. For two thousand years Israel has been in the land of her exile, and while there, as in the Book of Ruth, the Church is being called out. This is clearly seen in Acts 15. A question had arisen among the early Christians which greatly troubled them. After Paul had reported that the Gentiles were receiving Christ, the Hebrew Christians were reluctant to accept them unless they were circumcised and placed themselves under the law. If the Gentiles were admitted into the Church, then what about the promises of God to Israel concerning the Messianic Kingdom, and the restoration of the nation of Israel? Is God then all through with the nation of Israel? Has the Church taken Israel's place? Are we now spiritual Israel? And is the kingdom the Church? Will Israel never again be restored nationally to her full glory in her own land? Although this question was fully settled at this council in Acts 15 over nineteen hundred years ago, the great mass of Christendom has failed to understand the divine answer, and is still teaching, in the face of all prophecy and the evidence of history and the presence of Israel already in the land, that God is all done with the nation, and we (The Church) are now God's Kingdom people, and all the prophecies concerning Israel's restoration and blessing must be spiritualized and applied to the Church.

A Trick of Satan

This is just a trick of Satan to discredit the Word of God and make it unintelligible. Just so long as one fails to see the difference between Israel and the Church — the Kingdom and the Body of Christ, just so long will one grope about in a fog and close the door to the understanding of prophecy and make the Book of Revelation a dark, dark book of symbols, the study of which is to be carefully avoided. No man can understand God's program for this age until he sees clearly God's plan for Israel in the land and God's entirely different program for the Church as the heavenly Bride of Christ.

James' Answer

Now listen to James' answer to the question, "Is God all through with the nation of Israel?" The answer is clear and simple:

> And after they had held their peace, James answered, saying, Men and brethren, hearken unto me:
> Simeon hath declared how God at the first did visit the Gentiles, to take out of them a people for his name (Acts 15:13, 14).

Notice the revelation of this verse. God is first visiting the Gentiles to take out of them a people for His Name. That is what He is doing today. While Israel is rejected and scattered, God is calling out a people to be the Bride of Christ. While Naomi was a stranger in the land of Moab, God was calling out Ruth to be the future bride. And when that bride is complete, God will return Naomi to her land. And so James continues in Acts 15:15,

> And to this agree the words of the prophets; as it is written,
> After this I will return . . . (Acts 15:15, 16a).

After what? After God has completed calling out from the Gentiles His Church, then will He return, to restore the Kingdom of Israel:

> After this I will return, and will build again the tabernacle of David, which is fallen down; and I will build again the ruins thereof, and I will set it up (Acts 15:16).

Surely nothing can be clearer. First the Church is called out, while Israel is in exile from her land. After this the Lord will set up the kingdom. This is what Paul means when he says in Romans 11:

> For I would not, brethren, that ye should be ignorant of this mystery, lest ye should be wise in your own conceits; that blindness in part is happened to Israel, UNTIL the fulness of the Gentiles be come in.
> And so all Israel shall be saved: as it is written, There shall come out of Sion the Deliverer, and shall turn away ungodliness from Jacob (Rom. 11:25, 26).

We have almost reached that point. We are standing now where Naomi stood as she returned after nine years of distress in Moab. And Ruth is about to meet her lover, when Naomi returns to her land. Israel has heard the good news that there is bread again in Bethlehem and is returning to her homeland. Surely the longed-for day is almost here. Like Ruth, we are in the gleaning time of this dispensation and soon the day of harvest will be over. There is no time to be lost. Are you ready?

CHAPTER SIX

The Hour of Decision

THE story of the Gentile widow, Ruth, who became the beloved bride of the wealthy Jew, Boaz is a romance of love without peer or equal. A lovelier, sweeter romance has never been written in all literature, sacred or profane. Wholly apart from its inspired authorship and its deep spiritual meaning and infallible "Spirit-inspired" perfection, it still infinitely excels any novel which man has ever produced. We trust that you have read the four brief chapters again, for its lessons are inexhaustible.

In past chapters we have repeatedly pointed out that the family of Naomi is an unmistakable picture of the family of the nation of Israel. After dwelling in the land of milk and honey for centuries, they were, like Naomi's family, driven out by a famine under the judgment of God. They were scattered among the nations where they found a place of sorrow, distress, and death, until they were reduced to a mere handful of survivors. Naomi's family consisted of four persons, but soon after they reached Moab three of them had died and Naomi alone was left. Only 25 per cent of the original family survived. Moab became the place of graves in a strange land. One cannot mistake in all this the history of Naomi's nation, the children of Israel. God had said of them way back in Deuteronomy 4:27,

> And the LORD shall scatter you among the nations, and ye shall be left few in number among the heathen, whither the LORD shall lead you.

This is repeated in Deuteronomy 28:62,

> And ye shall be left few in number, whereas ye were as the stars of heaven for multitude; because thou wouldest not obey the voice of the LORD thy God.

History stands as irrefutable evidence of the divine truth of these prophetic words. The Nation today is almost 3500 years old, since they came out of Egypt as God's people. They have been one of the most prolific of all nations, yet have remained few in number compared to other nations, because of their persecutions and slaughter by their enemies. Beginning with Pharaoh who persecuted them in his effort to exterminate them by casting all boy babies into the river, the history of the nations has been a repetition of this Satanic attempt to destroy God's covenant people. Egypt, Babylon, Persia, Greece, Rome, Russia and Germany have all followed in the steps of Pharaoh, only to share Pharaoh's fate, and go under while the nation of Israel survived. At one time during the middle ages only one million of this nation remained. And today after 35 centuries of prolific increase, there are only about 18 million Jews in the world (1 per cent of the total population).

Naomi found in Moab a place of graves which almost wiped out her whole family. The sojourn of Israel among the nations is also pictured as a gigantic grave yard. Ezekiel sees a valley of dry bones scattered all over the valley. There were very many, and they were very dry. This was God's picture of Israel among the nations, for Ezekiel tells us definitely who they are:

> Then he said unto me, Son of man, these bones are the whole house of Israel: behold, they say, Our bones are dried, and

our hope is lost: we are cut off for our parts [our land] (Ezek. 37:11).

TO BE RESTORED

But they are not utterly to perish, but after the period of judgment they are to return to their land and be multiplied again. And so Ezekiel continues:

Therefore prophesy and say unto them, Thus saith the Lord GOD; Behold, O my people, I will open your graves, and cause you to come up out of your graves, and bring you into the land of Israel (Ezek. 37:12).

This resurrection of Israel has begun before our very eyes in the return of the nation politically to the land of Palestine. Yes, Naomi the widow, pining in Moab, has heard the good news from home, that there is bread in Judah, and is going back. Her decision to return to her homeland was prompted by the good news that the famine was ended and there was bread again in Judah. The famine in the land of Palestine had lasted for nineteen hundred years. Her mountains were bare, her valleys depleted, and one could hardly imagine a more barren desert land. And then, with the coming of the industrial revolution and the development of irrigation, the building of dams and power plants, the desert began to blossom as the rose. But most important of all in the past few decades, the rainfall in Palestine suddenly increased from a scant to an abundant volume. Agriculture made gigantic strides, industry began to hum, and this good news was heard by the nation in exile. In 1897 Theodor Herzl convened the first great Zionist Congress with the avowed purpose of interesting world Jewry in their ancient homeland and encouraging their return. Then in 1918 the Balfour Declaration gave added impetus to the movement, and when Britain received the mandate over Palestine, the migration was accelerated. Now with the recognition of the State of Israel in 1948, the time is here for the return home. Good news from home had awakened in the breast of Naomi an irrespressible nostalgia and homesickness for Bethlehem.

The Decision of Ruth

But Naomi was not to return alone, but bring with her a bride for her kinsman-redeemer Boaz, who was to restore to her the land which had been taken over by others during her absence.

> Wherefore she went forth out of the place where she was, and her two daughters in law with her; and they went on the way to return unto the land of Judah (Ruth 1:7).

Enter Ruth

Up until this time the narrative has dealt mainly with Naomi and her bereavement. Ruth is merely mentioned as the widow of Mahlon. But now comes the time for her to decide whether to abide in her pagan land of Moab with its idols and false gods, or to join Naomi, accept her Jehovah God, and go with her to the land of Judah. Bear in mind that Ruth represents prophetically the Church, the Bride of Christ; and Christ is typified by Boaz, the kinsman of Naomi.

An Important Decision

It was an important decision for Ruth to make, for her future destiny depended upon it. The record of her decision is deeply instructive.

> And Naomi said unto her two daughters in law, Go, return each to her mother's house: the LORD deal kindly with you, as ye have dealt with the dead, and with me.
>
> The LORD grant that ye may find rest, each of you in the house of her husband. Then she kissed them; and they lifted up their voice, and wept.
>
> And they said unto her, Surely we will return with thee unto thy people (Ruth 1:8-10).

Here are two young women standing before an important decision. Will they remain in their heathen idolatry, or will they make the journey with Naomi by faith, into a strange land? It must be a voluntary decision and act, and so Naomi answers them:

> Turn again, my daughters: why will ye go with me? are there yet any more sons in my womb, that they may be your husbands?
>
> Turn again, my daughters, go your way; for I am too old to have an husband. If I should say, I have hope, If I should have an husband also to night, and should also bear sons;
> Would ye tarry for them till they were grown? would ye stay for them from having husbands? nay, my daughters; for it grieveth me much for your sakes that the hand of the Lord is gone out against me (Ruth 1:11-13).

To understand this plea of Naomi for Ruth and Orpah to return, we must refer again to a law given by God to Israel. If a husband died without children, then the dead husband's brother was to take the widow and marry her and raise up a name for his dead brother. This law is described in detail in Deuteronomy 25, which we shall study in detail when we come to the redemption of Ruth in the following chapters.

Right here we merely mention the fact that Naomi reminds Orpah and Ruth that this would be impossible. The husbands of these two widows had no more brothers, and Naomi was too old to have more children. But even if Naomi could bear two more sons, these widows could hardly be expected to wait until they were grown. The argument convinced Orpah, and

> Orpah kissed her mother in law; but Ruth clave unto her (Ruth 1:14).

Orpah departs and is never mentioned again, but passes into oblivion. But not so with Ruth, for of her we read:
. . . but Ruth clave unto her (Ruth 1:14).

Ruth had learned about Naomi's God and was turning her back upon Moab and its idolatry, and leaves it all behind to become the bride of Naomi's kinsman Boaz.

In the following chapters we shall see the typical and prophetic meaning of the Gentile Ruth's decision to go with the Hebrew Naomi to her native land. But now before concluding this chapter, we would make a personal, practical application. Ruth is not only a picture of the Church, but also of the individual believer. Her sister-in-law, Orpah, had the same opportunity, but she turned back and is lost from view. Ruth decided for God and became an ancestor of the Lord Jesus Christ.

Orpah returned to her idolatry and is never mentioned again. It was all settled in one moment. It was her personal choice. But, oh, how much she lost by that one wrong decision! Her record ends in the darkness of heathen idolatry, but Ruth made the right choice of accepting Naomi's God and was rewarded by becoming the bride of the mighty, wealthy Boaz, and entered the line of the Redeemer of his people.

It Is Your Choice

Right this moment, if you are not a believer, you are facing this same important decision for eternity. By your first birth you like both Orpah and Ruth were born of Adam's accursed race, estranged from God and destined for the eternal darkness. But you too have been introduced to Naomi's God and right now you can decide either to receive the Lord Jesus Christ and be saved, or neglect to do so and be forever lost. Ruth said, "Thy God shall be my God, thy people shall be my people." From there on the Lord undertook to direct all her steps until she became the happy bride of Boaz, the redeemer.

What will your decision be today? Will you say, "Yes, I will leave the world and my old life, and go with God's people and become a member of the first family of heaven." Orpah went back into the gloom of Moabite darkness, pagan religion and final doom. She did not hate Naomi or Naomi's God. She loved Naomi but refused to receive Naomi's Redeemer. You too may be religious and travel for a time with God's people, but when the crisis comes and a decision *must* be made, the destiny of your soul is at stake.

Oh, like Ruth, make your decision today. "Believe on the Lord Jesus Christ, and thou shalt be saved."

CHAPTER SEVEN

Salvation Is of the Jews

So Naomi returned, and Ruth the Moabitess, her daughter in law, with her, which returned out of the country of Moab: and they came to Bethlehem in the beginning of barley harvest (Ruth 1:22).

God moves in a mysterious way,
His wonders to perform.

THIS is marvelously illustrated in the experience of the Hebrew widow, Naomi, and the Gentile widow, Ruth. Ruth was destined to become the wife of Boaz, the wealthy Jew of Bethlehem and kinsman of Naomi. But Naomi lived happily in Bethlehem and Ruth was a pagen maid in idolatrous Moab, ignorant of Israel's God and a stranger to the covenants of grace. How can this Gentile Ruth, and the wealthy Jewish land owner, Boaz, be brought together? Brought together they must be, for Ruth was destined to be an ancestor of the Redeemer, the Lord Jesus. God had a plan and a way by which these two could meet, become lovers, and marry. In order to do this, Naomi must be driven out by a terrible famine from her native land, and go to sojourn in the Gentile land of Moab. And here she carries the message of the true Jehovah, the one God of Israel. The Moabites were idol worshipers and were steeped in polytheism. They worshiped many gods. But Naomi was able while in Moab to interest her widowed daughter-in-law, Ruth, in the true God, so that when she returned to her land, Ruth had been won to Israel's God and returns to become the favored bride of her redeemer husband, Boaz. But in order to bring Ruth to Boaz, it was necessary for Naomi to be exiled from her land, bereft of her husband and her sons, and brought low before the Lord.

PROPHETIC PICTURE

One cannot fail to see clearly in this dealing of God with Naomi, in order to redeem Ruth, a picture of the scattering of the nation of Israel, and the calling out of the Bride, the Church, while Israel is banished from her land and pining among the nations. For 1500 years God dealt with one nation, the nation of Israel. The other nations were "Goyim," Gentile dogs, strangers to God, and outside the family of Jehovah. But God in His infinitely wise and foreknown plan had also made provision for the Gentiles that they might be saved. In order that they might be saved, the Lamb of God, the Messiah of Israel, the Lord Jesus, must be rejected, crucified, die and be raised. Without the death of the Lord Jesus there could be salvation for neither Jew nor Gentile.

And so God ordered His plan that when the Redeemer came He would be rejected. He must not be accepted by His people, for then they would not have crucified Him. The Cross would have been eliminated, the Kingdom would have been ushered in at that time, this age of grace would not have followed and no salvation for the world made possible. The Cross was a necessity in God's plan of redemption. It was planned from eternity. In Acts 15:18, in summing up God's rejection of Israel so the Church might also be brought in, we have James saying:

Known unto God are all his works from the beginning of the world.

God is omniscient. He knew everything from the beginning —from eternity. He knew every sparrow which would fall and the number of hairs on every person's head. He knew Adam would fall and bring death. He knew He would provide a salvation for fallen man. He knew beforehand that Israel would reject the Redeemer when He came and, as a result, the nation would be temporarily rejected and scattered throughout the earth. He planned it so. He ordered it thus. It could not have been different. It was God's way of carrying out His program of redemption for *all* men, and not one nation only.

HAD BEEN PROPHESIED

God not only foreknew, but also planned the rejection of the Messiah when He came 1900 years ago. If He had not been rejected it would have upset God's entire program, discredited God, and proven the Bible to be wrong. If this startles you, then remember that centuries before Christ came, God had already said that He would be rejected and slain by His own People. If then Israel had *not* rejected Him, God would be proven to have been mistaken and the Bible made a book of lies. No — in order that God's plans for the world might be accomplished, it was necessary for Israel to be blinded, and to be rejected for their unbelief.

Without wearying you with this profound subject, we do want to quote several Scripture passages to prove that God deliberately planned Calvary and the death of Christ at the hands of His people, in order to carry out His long-range program of redemption for the world. Listen to Isaiah, and God's commission to him:

And he said, Go, and tell this people, Hear ye indeed, but understand not; and see ye indeed, but perceive not.

Make the heart of this people fat, and make their ears heavy, and shut their eyes; lest they see with their eyes, and hear with their ears, and understand with their heart, and convert, and be healed (Isa. 6:9, 10).

This indeed was a strange commission. Isaiah is told to preach to the nation, but God tells him beforehand that they will not hear, or be converted by it. They will give no heed to it at all. And Isaiah seems to ask, "Then why preach to them if they will not hear? What's the use of wasting my breath?" And so he cries out in Isaiah 6:

Then said I, Lord, how long? And he answered, Until the cities be wasted without inhabitant, and the houses without man, and the land be utterly desolate.

And the Lord have removed men far away, and there be a great forsaking in the midst of the land (Isa. 6:11, 12).

To Isaiah's question, "How long will Israel reject the message?" — God says it will last until judgment falls, and they are scattered and removed from the land, and the land be forsaken. This was climaxed when Titus the Roman finally destroyed Jerusalem, killed and scattered its inhabitants, and sent them into dispersion for these past two millenniums.

But during this time of scattering, God will be gathering together another company, His Bride, from every people, tongue and tribe and nation, and then when the Bride is complete, God will begin to deal with Israel again. And so Isaiah 6:13 reads, after predicting this time of rejection:

But yet in it shall be a tenth, and it shall return, and shall be eaten: as a teil tree, and as an oak, whose substance is in them, when they cast their leaves: so the holy seed shall be the substance thereof.

All of this is illustrated for us in the Book of Ruth. The exile of Naomi was temporary. During her exile the family was reduced from four to one. Only a remnant returned; but before the return, Ruth had been prepared to meet the bridegroom. So too, says the Lord, Israel will remain in exile and the darkness of unbelief until the "fulness of the Gentiles" be come in, and then a remnant shall return to the land to be followed by the wedding of the Lamb.

As God drove Naomi from Bethlehem, that Ruth might be brought to Boaz, so God predicted and planned that Israel should also be set aside, while the Church, the Bride of Christ, was being prepared. That time seems very, very near with Naomi's people Israel already back in the land as a nation.

GOD IS SOVEREIGN

I realize many will object to the statement that God in His sovereignty made it impossible for Israel to receive her King, but there can be no other answer. Hundreds of years before, God had said they would not receive their King, and to prevent God from being mistaken and the Bible wrong, it must come to pass. In Isaiah 53:1 the prophet looking ahead to the coming of the Redeemer foresaw the certain rejection of Christ, and cried:

> Who hath believed our report? and to whom is the arm of the Lord revealed?

Isaiah clearly foresaw and foretold the rejection of the coming Redeemer, in spite of all the clear prophecies whereby He might be recognized. And the balance of the fifty-third chapter of Isaiah gives an unmistakable picture of the rejection and death and resurrection of the Lord Jesus. If, therefore, the Messiah were not rejected when He came, it would discredit all the prophecies of the Old Testament.

We might refer to scores of other prophecies, but we mention just one more, the twenty-second Psalm. In this Psalm we have a most complete prophetic picture of the suffering and death of the coming Saviour. It opens with the very words Jesus uttered on the Cross, "My God, My God, Why hast thou forsaken Me?" (Ps. 22:1), and then follows a detailed account of the suffering of Christ, the piercing of His hands and feet, the casting of lots upon His garments, His terrible thirst, and then His death. God foreknew all this, yea, He had planned it thus, that by the rejection of the Redeemer by His own nation, salvation might come to the Gentiles.

BACK TO NAOMI

All this is suggested by the experience of Naomi, representing Israel, driven from her land, and forsaken by God, that Ruth might be saved. In the prophetic application of this we see a striking parallel between the rejection of Israel by God, and the rejection of Jesus by the nation. Israel was rejected in order that the Gentiles might be saved. The nation became the vicarious sufferer that others might be brought in. Paul says in Romans 11:11, referring to the setting aside of the Nation, after they rejected the Saviour:

> I say then, Have they [Israel] stumbled that they should fall? God forbid: but rather through their [Israel's] fall salvation is come unto the Gentiles, for to provoke them to jealousy.

Through Israel's rejection, Christ went to the Cross, and by it God's plan of salvation was offered to all. But Israel shall be restored. Like the Lord Jesus, they died as a nation, and were buried among the Gentiles that God's salvation might come to all. But they will also be resurrected again, the dry bones shall live, and so Paul continues in Romans 11:12,

> Now if the fall of them [Israel] be the riches of the world, and the diminishing of them [Israel] the riches of the Gentiles; how much more their fulness?

All of this is also a picture of the Lord Jesus. He too was set aside and forsaken by God, and died that we might live. And He too arose and lives today as Redeemer and Saviour. Do you know Him? Have you like Ruth of old made your decision? The Cross of Christ blocks the road to hell. You can, if you will, choose to be lost, but it will be over the dead body of the Son of God and by wading through His precious blood. Oh, receive Him today, before it is too late.

CHAPTER EIGHT

Mysteries and Parables

> And it came to pass, when they [Naomi and Ruth] were come to Bethlehem that all the city was moved about them, and they said, Is this Naomi?
>
> And she said unto them, Call me not Naomi, call me Mara: for the Almighty hath dealt very bitterly with me.
>
> I went out full, and the Lord hath brought me home again empty: why then call ye me Naomi [the pleasant one], seeing the Lord hath testified against me, and the Almighty hath afflicted me? (Ruth 1:19-21)

THIS was Naomi's testimony after almost ten years of exile in the land of Moab. From her words we gather that she left the land under God's judgment in the mighty famine. The famine was sent by God in judgment, and Naomi now confesses, "the Lord hath testified against me, and the Almighty hath afflicted me." The famine which drove this Hebrew family out of Bethlehem to pine away in a strange land was not by accident or by chance. It was part of a fore-ordained plan; it was by the design of God. It was God who drove them out by sending a famine, and Naomi acknowledges now it was the Lord's doing, for she says:

> The Almighty hath dealt very bitterly with me.
>
> . . . seeing the Lord hath testified against me, and the Almighty hath afflicted me (Ruth 1:20, 21).

PICTURE OF ISRAEL

All of this becomes tremendously significant when we remember that in this entire story we have an unmistakable prophecy of the history of Naomi's people, the nation of Israel. Naomi must be banished from the land in order that Ruth, the Gentile widow might be brought to Boaz, the Redeemer of both Naomi and Ruth.

In the sovereign plan and purpose of God, Israel must reject her Messiah, and because of it, be dispersed among the nations, so that God's plan for the Church might also be carried out. The death of Christ at the hands of His people was foreordained and fixed. It could not have been otherwise, for God had foretold and prophesied it all beforehand. This is a great mystery to us with our finite minds, but it was no mystery with God. And so when Jesus was born in Bethlehem, He was born to die on the Cross. As surely as His birth was in God's plan, so surely was His death and resurrection.

MYSTERY OF THE AGES

When Christ came nearly 2,000 years ago, the people thought that He as the Messiah would immediately declare Himself King, throw off the Roman yoke, and bring in the glorious millennial reign of peace and righteousness. They did not see the mystery of the Church which must also be brought in. And so they asked Him, "Wilt thou at this time restore the kingdom to Israel?" His disciples even strove among themselves for prominent places in this kingdom. And then He made the shocking announcement that He would not set up the Kingdom at this time, but be rejected instead and as a result the nation of Israel would be judged, cast out of the land, and wander for centuries among the nations, where they would find a place of sorrow, tears, persecution and death. But by their rejection of the Redeemer, God's plan for both Israel and the Church would find its fulfillment. And so Jesus went to the Cross instead, rejected by His own, and Israel (like the family of Naomi) is set aside, while the Church (like Ruth) is being prepared for Her Husband. And then, when She is complete, God will again begin to deal with Israel, and bring her (like Naomi) back to the land, and restore to her the lost inheritance.

A Deep Mystery

This setting aside of the nation of Israel, while the Church Age runs its course, was a deep mystery, not made known in the Old Testament, but only fully revealed after Pentecost. Concerning this mystery, Paul says that he received the knowledge of this by special revelation:

> Which in other [the former] ages was not made known unto the sons of men, as it is now revealed unto his holy apostles and prophets by the Spirit;
> That the Gentiles [typified by Ruth] should be fellowheirs, and of the same body, and partakers of his promise in Christ by the gospel (Eph. 3:5, 6).

This was the mystery hidden until after Christ came. The word "mystery" is "mysterion" in the Greek, and comes from the root, "muo," which means "to be silent." It is taken from the secret password of Greek secret societies. Only those who knew the password as members of the exclusive order could enter in and know the secrets. All others remained in darkness.

How true this is of the mystery of the temporary rejection of Israel, and the mystery of the calling out of the Church, and the mystery of the final restoration of Israel for never-ending blessing in the land. Of it Paul says:

Now I would not, brethren, that ye should be ignorant of this mystery . . . that blindness in part is happened to Israel, UNTIL the fulness of the Gentiles be come in. And so all Israel shall be saved (Rom. 11:25, 26).

This is the mystery. Israel must be set aside as a nation during this dispensation. While she is set aside, God is calling out the Church. When the last one is added to the Body of Christ, the Messiah of Israel will return and restore her fully to her land and bring in the everlasting kingdom of peace and righteousness. Until Ruth is ready to become the bride of Boaz, Naomi must remain an exile in Moab.

This was an unknown thing (a mystery) to the Old Testament saints and Israel before the Cross. It is still a mystery to millions of Christians. Just so long as men teach that God is all through with Israel as a Nation, and the Church now has taken her place as spiritual Israel, just so long will they remain ignorant of the mystery of the ages, prophecy will be unintelligible and a subject to be carefully avoided, except for an occasional textual sermon of moral instruction and ethical application. The basic requisite for the proper understanding of prophecy is a knowledge of the difference between Israel and the Church, God's future plan for the Church and the Hebrew nation. Until this difference is clearly seen, men will continue to grope about in a thick fog of confusion.

Naomi does not surrender her position to Ruth. Ruth did not replace Naomi. She was merely banished for a time, until Ruth was ready to meet Boaz, and then she returned to be fully restored. Now this truth of this mystery was hidden by God from the nation, and God saw to it that they would not see it, so that His plan might be carried out, and Christ would be rejected and go to the Cross.

WHAT IS A PARABLE?

To carry out this divine purpose of God, Jesus deliberately spoke to the people of His day in such a way that they would not understand Him. He spoke this mystery of Israel and the Church in parables, totally unintelligible to the rejecters of Christ. In Matthew 13 we have Jesus giving the course of this mystery age from His first coming to His second coming. Beginning with the parable of the four soils, He ends up with the parable of the dragnet. This last parable is a picture of the end of this age. Jesus gave the explanation, for He says concerning the dragnet:

> So shall it be at the end of the world: the angels shall come forth, and sever the wicked from among the just,
> And shall cast them into the furnace of fire: there shall be wailing and gnashing of teeth (Matt. 13:49, 50).

But this remained a mystery to all except those whose eyes had been opened. Jesus therefore, spoke this prophecy of this present Church Age in the form of parables, for the deliberate purpose that they should not be able to understand it. Few people know what a parable is and why such were used. In Sunday school we were taught that a "parable is an earthly story with a heavenly meaning." Now that sounds pretty, but it says nothing. A parable is not merely an illustration. An illustration is designed to throw light on a subject. But a parable is the exact opposite. It is designed to hide the truth.

A parable may be defined as "that method of teaching whereby the truth will be completely hidden and veiled from some, while perfectly clear to others." Jesus spoke in parables to Israel in order to blind their eyes and keep them in darkness. Now I realize many of you are ready to challenge these statements and feel that I am completely mistaken.

But wait a moment, while we examine the record of the Word.

Matthew 13 is the great mystery chapter, containing seven mysteries spoken in parables. In verse 3 Matthew says —

> And he spake many things unto them in parables (Matt. 13:3).

And then follow the seven parables of the four soils, the tares, the mustard seed, the leaven, the hidden treasure, the pearl and the dragnet. The first four were spoken to the multitude; the last three were spoken privately to His disciples. After Jesus gave the first parable, the disciples were amazed and confused, and asked Him:

> Why speakest thou unto them in parables? (Matt. 13:10).

Now notice the answer of Jesus. He did not say, "I am trying to illustrate the truth so it will be easier for them to understand." Quite the contrary, He gives this astounding reply. He says He is using parables:

> Because it is given unto you to know the mysteries of the kingdom of heaven, but to them it is not given.
> Therefore speak I to them in parables: because they seeing see not, and hearing they hear not, neither do they understand.
> And in them is fulfilled the prophecy of Esaias, which saith, By hearing ye shall hear, and shall not understand; and seeing ye shall see, and not perceive:
> For this people's heart is waxed gross, and their ears are dull of hearing, and their eyes they have closed; lest at any time they should see with their eyes and hear with their ears, and should understand with their heart, and should be converted, and I should heal them (Matt. 13:11, 13-15).

If the nation had recognized their Redeemer, and received Him, He would not have gone to the Cross, and consequently, God's foreordained plan of redemption would have failed, the Bible proven untrue, and God a mistaken, unreliable deity, for He had foretold that they would reject Him. And so

God hid the truth from Israel in order to carry out His plan. In Matthew 13 this fact is further established:

> All these things spake Jesus unto the multitude in parables; and without a parable spake he not unto them:
> That it might be fulfilled which was spoken by the prophet, saying, I will open my mouth in parables; I will utter things which have been kept secret from the foundation of the world (Matt. 13:34, 35).

The mystery is revealed not to those who choose to see it, but only to those to whom God pleases to reveal it, and to all the rest it is hidden. Listen to Jesus again:

> At that time Jesus answered and said, I thank thee, O Father, Lord of heaven and earth, because thou hast hid these things from the wise and prudent, and hast revealed them unto babes.
> Even so, Father: for so it seemed good in thy sight (Matt. 11:25, 26).

You may rebel against this truth, and find fault with God, but God is sovereign and asks no man for counsel or advice. But if you are not yet convinced that the setting aside of Naomi's nation was predestined and it could not be otherwise, listen to the climaxing, clinching statement of Jesus in John 12:

> These things spake Jesus, and *departed, and did hide Himself* from them.
> But though he had done so many miracles before them, yet they believed not on him:
> That the saying of Esaias the prophet might be fulfilled, which he spake, Lord, who hath believed our report? and to whom hath the arm of the Lord been revealed?
> *Therefore they could not believe,* because that Esaias said again,
> He [God] hath blinded their eyes, and hardened their heart; that they should not see with their eyes, nor understand with their heart, and be converted, and I should heal them.

These things said Esaias, when he saw his glory and spake of him (John 12:36-41).

Isaiah saw the reason for the judicial blindness of Israel, so *they could not believe,* when he looked beyond into the future, and beheld the glory of the final consummation at the end, when Israel will be fully restored and the Church wedded to her Lord. Yes, God drove the family of Naomi out of Bethlehem that He might bring Ruth into the family. So God temporarily set aside the nation of Israel, that through her rejection salvation might come to all.

Understand this? No, but believe it — Yes! Do some of you, as you have read, say, "All this is a mystery to me; I cannot get anything out of it." Then ask God to open your eyes through faith in Christ, and you will find in this record, now so dry and dull, visions of truth which will take your breath away, and cause you to cry out with Paul:

O the depth of the riches both of the wisdom and knowledge of God! how unsearchable are his judgments, and his ways past finding out! (Rom. 11:33).

Except a man be born again, he cannot see . . . (John 3:3).

CHAPTER NINE

The Christian Debt to the Jew

THE Church of Jesus Christ is eternally indebted to the nation of Israel. The nation of Israel was chosen in sovereign grace to be the repository of divine revelation, a separated people through whom God would reveal the plan of redemption. It was from the nation of Israel that the Redeemer was born. The Bible, the Word of God, was written (with few exceptions) by members of this nation. How thankful we should be! But the greatest benefit the world received was a blessing which necessitated Israel's greatest tragedy. Israel must be set aside and banished from her land to pine away among the nations, in order to bring in the Bride of her Redeemer, the Church. We have seen this illustrated in the exile of Naomi's family from the land of Bethlehem, in order that through her exile, Ruth the Gentile bride might be prepared for and meet her husband, Boaz. But when Ruth was ready, Naomi returned to her former home. She did not become part of the Bride, nor was she left in exile. Nor did Ruth take Naomi's place. Her final restoration was more glorious than her former estate.

PICTURE OF ISRAEL

All this, we repeat again and again, is a picture of the nation of Israel, driven from her land, set aside for a time, while God's program for the Church is being completed. Failure to see this can only result in confusion concerning God's plan. Today the great mass of Christendom teaches that God is all through with Israel and is dealing exclusively with the Church. It teaches that because Israel rejected the Christ, God now has ended His national dealing with the nation and all of this in spite of the clearest revelation in the Word of God, and now with the nation back in her land after 2500 years of wandering.

ANSWER IN ROMANS

This error and sin against Israel was already being taught as far back as the days of the Apostle Paul. When the Gentiles were admitted into the early Church, men began to ask the question, "Is God through then with national Israel? Has the Church taken Israel's place? What then about all the prophecies concerning Israel's restoration in her land?" The question was brought up at the first church council in Jerusalem, and the verdict was, that after God had taken out from among the Gentiles a people for His name (the Church), He would again deal with the nation of Israel, and restore her completely (Acts 15:13-17).

In Romans, Paul devotes three whole chapters to the history of Israel (Romans 9, 10, and 11). He introduces these three chapters as an illustration to show God's faithfulness in keeping His promises to us, by reminding us of His dealing with the nation of Israel. In Romans 9 he rehearses God's past dealing with the nation in sovereign grace. In Romans 10 he reviews their present national rejection and shows how today there is no difference. While Israel is set aside as a nation, and the Church is being called out, both Jew and Gentile must be individually and personally saved by faith in Christ. There is no difference. There is only one way to be personally saved. In the interval between the first and second coming of Christ, Paul says:

For there is no difference, between the Jew and the Greek: for the same Lord over all is rich unto all that call upon him. For whosoever shall call upon the name of the Lord shall be saved (Rom. 10:12, 13).

But does not this imply that the difference between the Church and Israel has been done away with? Does not this mean that there is no separate plan for the Jews and for the Church? Yes, as far as personal salvation is concerned, there is no difference. The middle wall of partition is broken down (Eph. 2:14). But this does not mean that God's program for Israel *as a nation* has been canceled. It does not mean that all the prophecies concerning her glorious future must be spiritualized away. It does not mean that the Church has taken Israel's place. And so Paul opens Romans 11 with the question: If there is no difference between them today, and God is calling out the Church,

I say then, Hath God cast away his people? (Rom. 11:1)

There is the question. We are to face it, "Hath God cast away Israel as a nation forever?" Here is God's answer —

God forbid . . . God hath not cast away his people which he foreknew (Rom. 11:2).

Just because Israel rejected her Lord, God has not forsaken her. And then Paul refers to the time of Elijah when Israel under King Ahab had so far departed from their Jehovah King. Did God cast Israel off then? Ah, no — while He did bring judgment upon them, yet in grace He preserved the true remnant of Israel. God's covenant with Israel through Abraham, Isaac and Jacob was a covenant of grace and cannot be annulled by *works*. And then Paul plunges into the deep mystery of Israel's national blindness, and shows that the nation must be set aside for a purpose. They must reject the Messiah in order that Calvary might follow and salvation be made available to all the world. Listen to the argument:

> What then? Israel hath not obtained that which he seeketh for; but the *election* hath obtained it, and the *rest were blinded* (Rom. 11:7).

When the King came, only a small remnant recognized Him, because they were elected to see, but the rest of the nation were *blinded*, in order that they might lead Him to Calvary for the salvation of the world. They had to be smitten with blindness that others might see. Now do not question this, for Paul continues:

> (According as it is written, God hath given them [Israel] the spirit of slumber, eyes that they should not see, and ears that they should not hear;) until this day.
>
> And David saith, Let their table be made a snare, and a trap, and a stumblingblock, and a recompence unto them:
>
> Let their eyes be darkened, that they may not see, and bow down their back alway (Rom. 11:8-10).

Remember, these words were spoken of God's chosen nation. What is the reason for such seemingly arbitrary action? Did God call them only to reject them? Did He choose them that He might subsequently cast them off? Shall we accuse God of arbitrary injustice? Is God a God of caprice and sadism? Perish the thought! There was a plan in all this. Listen to the answer:

> I say then, Have they stumbled that they should fall? (Rom. 11:11).

Did God deliberately make them fall just to get rid of them and relieve Himself of carrying out His covenant with them? Hear the amazing answer:

> God forbid: but rather through their fall salvation is come unto the Gentiles, for to provoke them to jealousy (Rom. 11:11).

What a revelation! Through the fall of Israel, in rejecting their Messiah, *salvation is come to us Gentiles.* Our salvation was made possible by Israel's fall. They died as a nation that we might live. In the light of this, who can estimate the debt of gratitude every believer owes to Israel? God sacrificed as it were His ancient covenant people, in order to save us Gentiles. The believer who sees this truth can have nothing but love and compassion for the sons of Jacob. Anti-semitism is the most inconsistent and unreasonable thing for anyone who claims to be a Christian. It reveals a total lack of knowledge of the Bible and God's great plan. It is inconceivable that any true, born-again Christian can have aught but love and compassion for God's scattered people. A Jew-baiting Christian is a contradiction, an illogical monstrosity.

To Be Restored

But this is not the end of the story. Israel was not only set aside that we might be brought in, but she will also be rewarded for her sacrifice, and so Romans 11 continues:

> Now if the fall of them be the riches of the world, and the diminishing of them the riches of the Gentiles; how much more their fulness?
>
> For if the casting away of them be the reconciling of the world, what shall the receiving of them be, but life from the dead? (Rom. 11:12, 15).

The Tame Olive Tree

And then follows an illustration of the olive tree (Rom. 11:17-24). Israel is represented as a tame olive tree, rooted in the eternal covenant of God. Because of their unbelief the tame branches are cut off (Israel rejected and dispersed among the nations). During their rejection the branches of the wild olive tree (the Gentiles) are grafted into the stump. But ultimately the tame branches will be grafted in again (Israel as a nation will be restored).

> For if thou wert cut out of the olive tree which is wild by nature, and wert graffed contrary to nature into a good olive tree: how much more shall these, which be the natural branches, be graffed into their own olive tree? (Rom. 11:24)

Today the Church is being called out, while national Israel is set aside. But this will come to an end at God's appointed time, the Church will be complete and go to meet her Lord, and Israel's wanderings will cease and she will return to her land and her God, never to leave it again.

Naomi's exile was not forever. As soon as Ruth was prepared for her husband, Boaz, they returned to the land. And as far as the record goes, Naomi never left the land again. Paul clinches his argument for Israel's glorious restitution in these words:

> For I would not, brethren, that ye should be ignorant of this mystery, lest ye should be wise in your own conceits; that blindness in part is happened to Israel, UNTIL the fulness of the Gentiles be come in.
>
> And so all Israel shall be saved: as it is written, There shall come out of Sion the Deliverer, and shall turn away ungodliness from Jacob:
>
> For this is my covenant unto them, when I shall take away their sins (Rom. 11:25-27).

Yes, Israel's glorious future only awaits the completion of the program for the Church. When Ruth is ready, then will the program come to its glorious consummation. Before closing this marvelous chapter, Paul once more reminds us of the eternal debt the Gentiles owe to Israel. He says of Israel today:

> As concerning the gospel, they are enemies for your sakes: but as touching the election, they are beloved for the fathers' sakes.
>
> For the gifts and calling of God are without repentance (Rom. 11:28, 29).

Enemies for our sakes! Blinded that we might see, but still they are God's covenant nation, for God cannot repent of His promise to Abraham, Isaac and Jacob. The gifts and calling of God are not subject to change or repentance.

Once more the tremendous truth of Israel's rejection for our salvation is stated:

> Even so have these [Israel] also now not believed, that through your mercy they also may obtain mercy.
> For God hath concluded them [Israel] all in unbelief, that he might have mercy upon all (Rom. 11:31, 32).

Is it any wonder, as Paul saw this deep mystery, the vicarious sacrifice of the nation of Israel for the salvation of the world and their glorious restoration, he cries out in wonder, awe, adoration and worship:

> O the depth of the riches both of the wisdom and knowledge of God! how unsearchable are his judgments, and his ways past finding out!
> For who hath known the mind of the Lord? or who hath been his counsellor?
> Or who hath first given to him, and it shall be recompensed unto him again?
> For of him, and through him, and to him, are all things: to whom be glory for ever. Amen (Rom. 11:33-36).

CHAPTER TEN

The End of the Age

So Naomi returned, and Ruth the Moabitess, her daughter in law, with her, which returned out of the country of Moab: *And they came to Bethlehem in the beginning of the barley harvest* (Ruth 1:22).

NAOMI who had been driven from Bethlehem because of a famine in the house of bread, is now returning after almost ten years of exile. During her banishment from home she had suffered unspeakable tragedy and bereavement, but she had gained a daughter. Ruth the Moabitess returns with Naomi. We have seen how closely Naomi's experience foreshadowed the history of her nation Israel. Israel too left her land wasted and spoiled, to sojourn for centuries among the nations. During Israel's rejection God is calling out a Bride for Naomi's Redeemer and Messiah; and then when the good news came that there was bread in Bethlehem, she returns to the land.

TIME OF HARVEST

We come now to another interesting and significant detail in the story. The return of Naomi and Ruth was in the beginning of the *harvest*. It was the time of reaping toward the end of the season. The sowing time was past, and the time for the final reaping had come. Soon the time for threshing would be here and the rejoicing of the harvest festival. The time of Naomi's return is significant, as well as the gleaning of Ruth till the end of the harvest.

Jesus said in His parable of the wheat and the tares:

The harvest is the end of the world [age] (Matt. 13:39).

Literally this reads, "The harvest is the consummation of the age." It was at the time of harvest that Naomi returns to her land. Surely we cannot fail to see in this a prophecy of the time when Israel will return from her exile, and come back to her homeland. Remember Naomi came back during the harvest time and the harvest is the end of the age of her exile. After centuries of wandering Israel has just recently returned to her native Judea. It is an unmistakable sign of the end of the age. It is the time of the final harvesting, and as we shall see in the experience of Ruth, the gleaning time for the Church.

Of all the signs of the imminent return of the Lord, there is none more significant than the return of Israel to Palestine in the last decade. When Jesus answered the question of the disciples:

Tell us, when shall these things be? and what shall be the sign of thy coming, and the end of the world [age]? (Matt. 24:3)

He gave a large number of signs in this lengthy chapter, and right in the midst of the discourse He says:

Now learn a parable of the fig tree; When his branch is yet tender, and putteth forth leaves, ye know that summer is nigh:

So likewise ye, when ye shall see all these things, know that it is near, even at the doors.

Verily I say unto you, This generation [the people of Israel] shall not pass, till all these things be fulfilled (Matt. 24:32-34).

The fig tree is Israel, withered because it had leaves but no fruit when the Lord looked for figs. It was withered *from* the roots. The root remained, like the olive tree of Romans 11, whose branches only were cut off. And this living stump will sprout again, and Jesus says when you see this withered fig tree (Israel) coming to life, "Then know that My coming is nigh, even at your doors." Surely the fig tree has come to life, and is indeed putting forth leaves. Israel is alive again as a nation. The return of the nation is an unmistakable sign that the harvest is here and the harvest is the end of the age.

NOT YET RESTORED

But while Naomi returned with Ruth to Bethlehem at the time of the harvest, she did not receive back her lost estate. During the years of Naomi's exile she had lost claim to her property which she had left. It had fallen into the hands of strangers. To have it restored to her again a Redeemer must be found. But this redemption does not occur until after the harvest is ended and the night of threshing out the wheat has passed. Then in the morning, after the wheat has been separated from the chaff, Boaz appears to take Ruth as his bride and to restore the lost land to the family of Naomi.

TRUE TO THE TYPE

In the recent return of the nation of Naomi, we have witnessed the fulfillment of this wonderful picture in the Book of Ruth. Israel is back in the land, but is not yet in possession of all she has lost. Only a fraction of the original grant of Canaan is in the hands of Israel, and even Jerusalem is still largely in the hands of the Arabs. But she is back in the land as a nation and soon the harvest of this age will be over and the last gleanings will be gathered in. Then will follow the night of the threshing time of the great Tribulation, to be followed by the morning, the wedding of the Church, and the final establishment of blessing for Israel in the land.

ENTER BOAZ

This redemption was accomplished by a kinsman of Naomi. And so Boaz, the chief actor in the drama of Ruth, is introduced. After the account of Naomi's return at harvest time, we read:

> And Naomi had a kinsman of her husband's, a mighty man of wealth, of the family of Elimelech; and his name was Boaz (Ruth 2:1).

The name, Boaz, means "In him is the strength." He is to become the redeemer of Naomi's lost estate, and the husband of the widow Ruth. How all this was brought about in the providence of God is a story of deepest human interest and beauty. Naomi and Ruth are both poverty-stricken upon their arrival in Bethlehem. They have nothing and so employment must be found. Naturally it would fall upon the younger of the two to go and seek for food.

RUTH THE GLEANER

There was just one thing Ruth was permitted to do. She was too poor to buy food, but according to the law she was allowed to glean in the fields and retain whatever she found behind the reapers. In Leviticus 19 we read God's provision for the poor:

> And when ye reap the harvest of your land, thou shalt not wholly reap the corners of thy field, neither shalt thou gather the gleanings of thy harvest.
>
> And thou shalt not glean thy vineyard, neither shalt thou gather every grape of thy vineyard; thou shalt leave them for the poor and stranger: I am the LORD your God (Lev. 19:9, 10).

Evidently Ruth was familiar with this provision, having most likely been informed about this law by Naomi. And so Ruth accepts the dole.

> And Ruth the Moabitess said unto Naomi, Let me now go to the field, and glean ears of corn after him in whose sight I shall find grace. And she said unto her, Go, my daughter. And she went, and came, and gleaned in the field after the reapers: and her hap was to light on a part of the field belonging unto Boaz, who was of the kindred of Elimelech (Ruth 2:2, 3).

How wonderful the provision God had made for the stranger Ruth! How marvelous His leading to bring her to her future husband, Boaz! God had given access to the stranger to glean in another's field. In Deuteronomy 24 God had said:

> When thou cuttest down thine harvest in thy field, and hast forgot a sheaf in the field, thou shalt not go again to fetch it: it shall be for the stranger, for the fatherless, and for the widow: that the LORD thy God may bless thee in all the work of thine hands.
>
> When thou beatest thine olive tree, thou shalt not go over the boughs again: it shall be for the stranger, for the fatherless, and for the widow.
>
> When thou gatherest the grapes of thy vineyard, thou shalt not glean it afterward: it shall be for the stranger, for the fatherless, and for the widow (Deut. 24:19-21).

GRACE! GRACE! GRACE!

What a picture of the grace of God to those who are poor and needy! The stranger had no inheritance in the land, but in condescending grace God made provision whereby they might be partakers of the harvest. The land in which Ruth gleaned belonged to Boaz the Jew. Ruth the Gentile had no claim to it by herself. But by the grace of God she became a partaker. God made His covenant of grace with Abraham. The other nations were excluded and were Gentile dogs. But by the grace of God, we, because of our Great Boaz, the Lord Jesus, the Lord of the harvest, have been invited into the family of God.

Ruth recognized the grace of Boaz and gladly accepted it. As she began gleaning in the field of Boaz, the lord of the harvest came by and his eyes fell on the beautiful stranger. After inquiry he learns her identity and being a close relative of Naomi's husband, he befriends her, encourages her, and gives her full liberty to glean wherever she would. Overcome with gratitude, we read:

> Then she fell on her face, and bowed herself to the ground, and said unto him, Why have I found grace in thine eyes, that thou shouldest take knowledge of me, seeing I am a stranger? (Ruth 2:10).

Ruth recognized that Boaz had gone far beyond the provisions of the law in bestowing grace upon her. And so Ruth gleaned happily in the field of her lord until the day was done. Our story says:

> So she gleaned in the field until even, and beat out that she had gleaned: and it was about an ephah of barley (Ruth 2:17).

And when the night came, the dark night of threshing, she rested safely and sweetly at the feet of Boaz, to become his bride in the morning. This we shall elaborate upon later, but now before the close of this chapter, we would see the wonderful prophetic lesson. Ruth is a stranger, an alien from the covenants of Israel. By grace she is permitted to glean in the field of Boaz. Boaz is a picture of Christ the Redeemer. Ruth is a picture of the Bride of Christ. The field is the world; the harvest is the end of the age; the sheaves are the children of men who are gathered and won to Christ by Ruth, the Church. The evening is coming on and soon the dark night will fall, when the threshers shall beat the sheaves to separate the chaff from the wheat. The tares and chaff will be burned, the wheat gathered into the barn.

We are living in the gleaning time of the harvest which

is the end of this age. Soon the day of reaping will be over. Then will follow the dark night of earth's greatest sorrow and tribulation, the day of the Lord, the dark night of threshing. But during that night the Church will be resting safely and securely at the feet of her Lord. Like Ruth, she will be in His presence till the indignation be past. Soon we shall hear His voice saying:

> Come my people, enter thou into thy chambers, and shut thy doors about thee: hide thyself as it were for a little moment, until the indignation be overpast (Isa. 26:20).

One of these days the door will be shut, making safe those who are inside, but forever closing the door of salvation to those who are outside. It is still the day of grace. It is not yet too late. The door is still open. Will you enter in?

CHAPTER ELEVEN

Handfuls on Purpose

And Ruth the Moabitess said unto Naomi, Let me now go to the field, and glean ears of corn after him in whose sight I shall find grace . . .

And she went, and came, and gleaned in the field after the reapers: and her hap was to light on a part of the field belonging unto Boaz . . .

Then said Boaz unto Ruth, Hearest thou not, my daughter? Go not to glean in another field, neither go from hence, but abide here fast by my maidens:

So she gleaned in the field until even (Ruth 2:2,3,8,17).

A GLEANER is one who follows the reapers, to gather up the stray stalks of grain which have been passed by as the reapers tied the sheaves into bundles. First the reapers with their sickles would cut the grain, handful by handful, until they had enough for a bundle or a sheaf, and then they would tie it together to be brought to the threshing floor. The gleaning is at the end of the harvest, and when the gleaning is finished, the harvest is ended.

The harvest is the end of the age. The stalks of grain are the souls of men to be won for Christ, separated from the chaff and gathered into the heavenly home. The field is the world. Jesus is the Lord of the harvest. The Church is engaged today in picking up the gleanings here and there and soon the fullness of the Gentiles will be brought in, and Christ shall come to call the Church home to rest at His feet during the threshing night of the Tribulation. And then will come the morning of the wedding day of the Church and her Lord.

TIME TO GLEAN

For nineteen hundred years the Church has labored in the Lord's harvest fields, and now we are in the gleaning time of this age. It is not as easy to win men and women for Christ as in days gone by. From thousands of pastors and evangelists we hear the complaint that conversions are fewer and more difficult. Where before dozens and scores responded, now it is one here and one there. Many are disappointed and some almost despairing. And then God gives a refreshing, a revival, to encourage His fainting reapers.

In the story of Ruth we have a beautiful incident of how God encourages His people lest they become weary. How graciously and tenderly Boaz makes provision for the gleaner Ruth in her arduous and wearying task. He provides for her food and drink and sustenance. Hear the gracious Boaz speaking to the lonely Ruth:

> At mealtime come thou hither, and eat of the bread, and dip thy morsel in the vinegar. And she sat beside the reapers: and he reached her parched corn, and she did eat, and was sufficed, and left (Ruth 2:14).

One sees more than a mere personal interest in the welfare of a poor widow in this gracious consideration by Boaz. There is evidence here of a love which was to blossom forth into full romance and a beautiful wedding. Remembering that Boaz is a picture of our Redeemer Christ, and Ruth a picture of the Church, His bride to be, we see in this gracious gesture of Boaz a wonderful illustration of our Saviour's love and personal attention to the least and lowliest individual. Ruth was a stranger, an outcast by birth, just a servant girl gleaning behind the reapers, but she was not overlooked by the lord of the harvest. The reapers may scarcely have noticed Ruth, and others may overlook her, but Boaz observed her every move and rewarded her for her faithfulness.

PERSONAL ATTENTION

What a comfort this should be to the many of God's dear children who must labor in the forgotten places, who must do the menial tasks, and go unobserved by the multitude. The reapers were the prominent ones in the eyes of the observers. Many were the shouts of encouragement as they cut down sheaf after sheaf of golden grain. Great was the applause at their skill in handling the sickle and the dexterity with which they neatly tied up the grain in securely bound bundles. But the gleaners (who represented the poor and the stranger and the widows) received but scant attention, as with aching back and chapped hands they picked a stalk here and a stalk there.

But there was one who did not overlook the poor gleaners. It was Boaz, the lord of the harvest. He knew the wearisome task of the scant gleanings while others brought in the sheaves. And he has a special encouragement for these obscure but faithful laborers. He says, "Take your place with the reapers, eat the same food they do, and dip in the same vinegar." You shall share in the same reward, for the Lord of the fields rewards for faithfulness, no matter how menial the task may be. The faithful gleaners shall receive the same reward as the faithful reapers.

WHAT A COMFORT

Surely this is encouraging. Not all God's children are privileged to be reapers. Some can only glean a loose ear here and another there. Some have but one talent, and have not been given the gift of being able to wield the sickle. I am thinking of the thousands of unknown gleaners in God's harvest, the faithful preachers in the out of the way places, the Sunday school teachers in some isolated, abandoned country schoolhouse, the invalided, bedridden sufferer who can only pray, the humble servant of Christ who can only give out a tract. These, though only gleaners, have a part in the harvest, and when we shall sit down at the Supper of the Lamb, these too will hear the Lord of the Harvest say, as Boaz said to Ruth:

> The LORD recompence thy work, and a full reward be given thee of the LORD God of Israel, under whose wings thou art come to trust.
>
> . . . come thou hither, and eat of the bread, and dip thy morsel in the vinegar. And she sat beside the reapers (Ruth 2:12,14).

Heaven will be a place of many surprises, I am sure, and one of them will be to find the full and complete story of the forgotten gleaners in God's harvest field. The gleaners could not report large numbers of sheaves which they had reaped, but the reapers were not done until the gleaners were through. There will be no "big shots" in heaven. When the books are opened up there, we shall find many, many whom the world never recognized or even heard about, shining in the glory of their great reward, while many who here below rode the crest of popular acclaim and basked in the limelight of popularity, will have to take a lower seat, for the "first shall be last, and the last shall be first."

God does not overlook faithfulness in the lowest and humblest place of service. All over this land and throughout the world are men and women, boys and girls, laboring and struggling with but few talents, under adverse conditions in the obscure places, picking up a stalk of grain here and another there. They go unnoticed and unsung, but what a revelation it will be, when the Lord of the Harvest calls them to sit with Him at the head of the table near to Himself. That was where Ruth sat at the table of Boaz. She sat right next to him, between Boaz and the reapers. This is quite evident, for we read in Ruth 2:14:

> And she sat beside the reapers: and he [Boaz] reached her parched corn, and she did eat and was sufficed, and left.

Yes, when Jesus comes, you forgotten souls who have only had the task of gleaning will have your day. You faithful ones who feel your task is so unimportant, you who can only do a little, you who pray and weep, you who labor in the hard place in that little field, your reward is sure. Remember, God rewards faithfulness rather than success.

> It is required in stewards, that a man be found faithful (I Cor. 4:2).

HANDFULS ON PURPOSE

But we do not have to wait until we get to heaven before we receive our reward, for the Lord also knows how much we need encouragement along the way, here and now. Notice how Boaz provided encouragement for poor Ruth:

> And when she was risen up to glean, Boaz commanded his young men, saying, Let her glean even among the sheaves, and reproach her not:
> And let fall also some of the handfuls of purpose for her, and leave them, that she may glean them, and rebuke her not (Ruth 2:15, 16).

HANDFULS ON PURPOSE! How perfectly wonderful. Boaz commanded his reapers to deliberately let fall whole handfuls of grain to encourage poor Ruth. This was designed to keep her from becoming disheartened, if the gleanings seemed sparse and scant. Yes, the Lord still drops handfuls on purpose along the way. Just when we begin to wonder why our ministry seems so barren, God sends a revival, a handful on purpose. I believe that the revivals in the history of the Church are not only for the purpose of winning souls, but also for the encouragement of the Church. When things become difficult, and it seems that everything is going to pot and ruin, God raises up His man to be used for a reviving of God's people. They are "handfuls on purpose" to assure us that God sees our struggles and is still on the throne.

THE END OF THE AGE

Today we are in the gleaning time of the dispensation. The harvest is almost over and only the gleanings seem to be left. We have heard much about the increase of crime and violence, unbelief and apostasy. For years now we have observed the increasing difficulty of interesting men and women in the Gospel. Pastors and evangelists and Christian workers had become discouraged and despondent at the meager results and then God drops for us a "handful on purpose." It was so in the days of Finney, and Wesley and Whitefield and Moody and Billy Sunday, and today, thank God, in a Billy Graham. Amid the deepening gloom God is giving us a handful on purpose, dropping a whole bunch of blessing to prove He is still the Lord of the Harvest.

It may be the last handful on purpose, for the harvest is drawing to a close. This is no time to relax, but rather to renew our zeal to bring them in. Whether you are one of the reapers, privileged of God to harvest arms full of sheaves, and see thousands come to Christ, or whether you are one of the gleaners, the Lord of the Harvest will reward you according to your faithfulness. We read of Ruth:

So she gleaned in the field until even (Ruth 2:17).

She gleaned until even — until nightfall, and was rewarded by spending the night at Boaz' feet and becoming his bride in the morning. It is evening and the shadows are falling over the field of this world.

And then the threshing time, when after the Church is caught away with her Lord, He will thresh the nations, separate the chaff from the wheat, and burn the tares with unquenchable fire. But today is still harvest time. Soon will come the winnowing time of judgment, and then for all who reject now, it will be forever too late.

CHAPTER TWELVE

The Pretribulation Rapture

THE harvest in the fields of Bethlehem has come to an end, and the time for threshing and winnowing the grain is at hand. Ruth, the Gentile, Moabitish widow, had been busy ever since the return of Naomi to Bethlehem, gleaning in the field of a wealthy Jew by the name of Boaz. He had shown her many, many favors and befriended this poor, impoverished, servant girl. And now the harvest is done and the night comes on. Is this to be the end of the affair with Boaz? Are they now to part and see each other no more? Will Ruth be compelled to seek employment elsewhere and will Boaz forget all about the attractive stranger from Moab?

NAOMI HAS A PLAN

These were evidently questions which Naomi the widowed mother-in-law was turning over in her mind, until she formulated and proposed a most daring plan to assure the continuance of the budding romance. To the unspiritual mind the suggestion of Naomi will seem vulgar, but to the spiritual man it is one of the most wonderful revelations of the love of God. This is Naomi's suggestion and advice to Ruth:

> Then Naomi her mother in law said unto her, My daughter, shall I not seek rest for thee, that it may be well with thee?
>
> And now is not Boaz of our kindred, with whose maidens thou wast? Behold, he winnoweth barley tonight in the threshingfloor.

Wash thyself therefore, and anoint thee, and put thy raiment upon thee, and get thee down to the floor: but make not thyself known unto the man, until he shall have done eating and drinking.

And it shall be, when he lieth down, that thou shalt mark the place where he shall lie, and thou shalt go in, and uncover his feet, and lay thee down; and he will tell thee what thou shalt do.

And she said unto her, All that thou sayest unto me I will do.

And she went down unto the floor, and did according to all that her mother in law bade her.

And when Boaz had eaten and drunk, and his heart was merry, he went to lie down at the end of the heap of corn: and she [Ruth] came softly, and uncovered his feet, and laid her down.

And she lay at his feet until the morning (Ruth 3:1-7, 14).

NAOMI THE MATCHMAKER

To the unspiritual mind this suggestion of Naomi was entirely out of place, but when we understand the motive and the faith of Naomi it becomes the story of a faith that would not be denied. After the harvest was ended, the sheaves were brought to the threshingfloor to be winnowed. This was done at night to get the advantage of the night breezes which sprang up after dark in that country and which were needed to successfully fan the grain, to separate it from the chaff. The grain would first be beaten out of its husk and separated from the straw. Then the grain was picked up and cast up into the wind. The heavier grain would fall onto the threshingfloor, while the lighter chaff would be blown away. After the grain had been thus winnowed and the winds subsided about midnight, a sumptuous meal was served and then all retired.

The owner of the grain would then remain on the scene and

lie down at the side of the heap of winnowed grain to guard
it against thieves who would otherwise steal it. And so Boaz
after the meal lay down at the pile of grain. Naomi was fully
familiar with this harvest and threshing routine, and so she
instructed Ruth to wait until the lights were all out, and the
floor was quiet, and then to steal softly to the place where
Boaz was sleeping, uncover his feet and lie down.

Was This Vulgar?

On the surface it sounds daring and bold, if not downright
vulgar. It might be mistaken as solicitation and ruin the
whole plan. But it was nothing of the sort. Ruth was acting
wholly within her legal rights and her conduct was entirely
proper. Naomi knew all this, for she was familiar with the
word of the Lord, and God's redemption plan for poor widows
like Ruth. In Deuteronomy 25:5 God had commanded:

> If brethren dwell together, and one of them die, and have
> no child, the wife of the dead shall not marry without unto
> a stranger: her husband's brother shall go in unto her, and take
> her to him to wife, and perform the duty of an husband's broth-
> er unto her.
>
> And it shall be, that the firstborn which she beareth shall
> succeed in the name of his brother which is dead, that his
> name be not put out of Israel (Deut. 25:5, 6).

Evidently Naomi was familiar with this provision and had
communicated it to Ruth. Boaz was a near kinsman, probably
a brother of Naomi's husband. According to the law it was
his duty, since he was still single, to marry the widow of
Mahlon, son of Naomi. Ruth by her action was only taking
the initiative to remind Boaz of his obligation to her. She did
not have to wait for Boaz to bring up the matter. It was
perfectly proper for the widow to do so and remind the
kinsman of his duty since God had commanded it.

BOAZ UNDERSTOOD

And Boaz understood it as well, and accepted his responsibility. Notice his action:

> And it came to pass at midnight, that the man was afraid, and turned himself: and, behold, a woman lay at his feet.
> And he said, Who art thou? And she answered, I am Ruth thine handmaid: spread therefore thy skirt over thine handmaid; for thou art a near kinsman (Ruth 3:8,9).

Ruth reminds Boaz she is there only because he is the kinsman whose duty it is to redeem her widowhood, and Boaz accepts the responsibility.

> And he said, Blessed be thou of the LORD . . .
> . . . fear not; I will do to thee all that thou requirest: . . .
> And now it is true that I am thy near kinsman:
> Tarry this night, and it shall be in the morning . . . then will I do the part of a kinsman to thee, as the LORD liveth: lie down until the morning.
> And she lay at his feet until the morning (Ruth 3:10-14).

And when the morning came Boaz fulfilled his promise. On this we shall deal at length later. But now we would remind you again that all this has also a prophetic meaning. Naomi, as Israel, is back in the land. Ruth, the future bride of Boaz, is gleaning in the field, a beautiful picture of the Church in the world, gleaning sheaves for the Master. But soon the harvest will end and the dark night of the Tribulation will descend upon the world. It will be the time of threshing of the nations, the day of God's judgment upon a wicked world. It will be a time of separating the wheat, the true Israel from the chaff. Jesus Himself said the harvest is the end of the age, and in His parable of the dragnet in Matthew, He foretells the final separation of the good from the bad.

But during that awful night of earth's greatest darkness and sorrow the Church will be safely resting at her Lord's feet.

We believe we are living in the very last days before God's judgment will fall upon a Christ-rejecting nation and a Christ-rejecting world. Jesus says of this terrible night:

> For then shall be great tribulation, such as was not since the beginning of the world to this time, no, nor ever shall be.
> And except those days should be shortened, there should no flesh be saved: but for the elects' sake those days shall be shortened (Matt. 24:21, 22).

But before that day comes, Christ will catch His Church away to a place of safety. Believer, are you ready to meet your Lord? He may call at any moment, "Come and enter into thy chambers and hide thyself for a moment, until the indignation be overpast." If we really believe this, we will prepare ourselves to meet Him. Notice, therefore, the advice Naomi gave to Ruth. She seems to say, You are going now to meet your future husband, and you must look your very best, clean and sweet and pure and beautiful. Here are Naomi's exact words, and I trust you will see how appropriate they are:

> Wash thyself therefore, and anoint thee, and put thy raiment upon thee, and get thee down to the floor (Ruth 3:3).

Wash, anoint, dress up, for the great occasion. Get rid of all which contaminates or stains, smell with the sweetest perfume, and put on your best clothes. You are going to meet your husband! Until this moment in Ruth's life, Ruth had evidently still been dressed in her widow's weeds. She had worn the badge of mourning in respect for the dead. She is to lay aside the last reminder of her unhappy experience in the land of Moab. She is now to break the last thread that might bind her to her former land, associates, and friends. The last tie with the old life is broken. She is now free and ready to meet her husband, and so she puts on her beautiful robes of joy and hope. They are the garments she will wear at the wedding.

Are you dressed to meet your Lord who may come at any moment? Are you washed and clean, or are you still stained with some worldly habit or fleshly lust? And how do you smell? Is it the sweetness of a sanctified spirit, or do you carry the stench of the onions, leeks and garlic of Egypt on your spiritual breath?

And how are you dressed? In the smelly grave clothes like Lazarus, when he came forth from the tomb, or are your garments white and clean? If the Lord should come today, how would He find you?

CHAPTER THIRTEEN

Kissing the Bride

And Naomi had a kinsman of her husband's, a mighty man of wealth, of the family of Elimelech; and his name was Boaz (Ruth 2:1).

THIS man, Boaz, who plays the chief role in the beautiful story of Ruth was an unusual and a remarkable man. Several things are to be noted in this first verse which mentions Boaz. First, he was a near relative of Naomi's dead husband. Second, he was a mighty man, probably referring to his great influence and high standing in the community. Third, he was a very wealthy man who was owner of the harvest fields in which Ruth found a place to glean. Furthermore, he was a most gracious personality, for he spared no effort to make a poor, widowed, Gentile maid feel at home in a strange land. Moreover, he was a liberal soul, for he loaded Ruth down with fruits for which she had not labored. In Ruth 3:15 we read:

Bring the veil that thou hast upon thee, and hold it. And when she held it, he measured six measures of barley, and laid it on her: and she went into the city.

This was a reward for Ruth's faithfulness in reminding Boaz of his duty as a kinsman. Ruth had, upon the advice of her mother-in-law Naomi, taken the daring step of slipping, under cover of darkness, into the bedchamber of Boaz and lying down at his feet while he was fast asleep. This was not a sinful act, or presumptuous boldness, but an act of faith in the man, Boaz. She merely reminds him of his duty as a kinsman. That Boaz recognizes it as such is seen from his reaction. There in the darkness of the threshingfloor he speaks tenderly to her and assures her of his love for her, and promises, that come the morning, he will immediately take steps to redeem both Naomi's inheritance and Ruth's widowhood. Listen to his kind words at midnight:

> And now, my daughter, fear not; I will do to thee all that thou requirest: for all the city of my people doth know that thou art a virtuous woman.
>
> And now it is true that I am thy near kinsman: howbeit there is a kinsman nearer than I.
>
> Tarry this night, and it shall be in the morning, that if he will perform unto thee the part of a kinsman, well; let him do the kinsman's part: but if he will not do the part of a kinsman to thee, then will I do the part of a kinsman to thee, as the LORD liveth: lie down until the morning (Ruth 3:11-13).

WHY GO TO BOAZ?

Here a question arises. Why did not Ruth present herself to the nearer kinsman rather than to Boaz? There was a nearer relative to Naomi, whose first duty would have been to redeem both Naomi and Ruth, but instead Naomi ignores him completely and sends Ruth to Boaz. Evidently Naomi knew that the other kinsman was unable to redeem, and so passes him by completely. This will become clear as we move on into the last chapter.

Naomi the matchmaker had sent Ruth to the threshingfloor with the express purpose of getting Ruth married to Boaz. That was the aim of the whole scheme. For this reason she had instructed her daughter:

> Wash thyself therefore, and anoint thee, and put thy raiment upon thee (Ruth 3:3).

Ruth was to go to Boaz that night dressed as a bride for a wedding. Her dress included a veil. It was probably her wedding veil, or it may have been the widow's veil, or the ordinary veil worn by women in the orient. The point is this: Boaz asked her to remove the veil for him. Such an act of intimacy was proper only to one who was to be her husband. It was a symbol of marriage, much as the bridegroom at the marriage ceremony lifts the veil of the bride to give her the wedding kiss. That night on the threshingfloor of Boaz, between the end of the harvest and the morning of the wedding day, time was spent in discussing their coming marriage.

And then as the night ended Boaz filled her veil with barley as a gift. She had not labored for it; it was a reward of love for faithfulness. And then the morning came, and Ruth returns to her mother-in-law.

> And when she came to her mother in law, she said, Who art thou, my daughter? (Ruth 3:16a)

We are to stop here and consider the strange question of Naomi, "Who art thou?" Didn't Naomi know her own daughter-in-law? Ah, yes, but the question implied something else. She really asked, "What is your name now? Has it been changed? Are you to be Mrs. Boaz? Who are you now?" And then Ruth assures her that everything had gone well, and:

> She told her all that the man had done to her (Ruth 3:16b).

It was the assurance that she was to be the happy bride. Then she showed her the gift of barley as a token of his favor. The engagement had taken place. Ruth is now in the eyes of God already the wife of Boaz. It only awaits legal ratification before the elders and the people of Bethlehem. This will be immediately completed.

Our Coming Bridegroom

All this, we remind you again, becomes an unmistakable picture of the love of our Redeemer Christ for His happy bride, the Church. We are still in the gleaning days of the age, and the night is drawing near when the Lord of the harvest will thresh the nations of the earth in the day of God's wrath and tribulation. Every indication about us points to the imminency of earth's judgment. All the signs of the end of the age and the return of the Lord are present today. Deception, wars, rumors of wars, pestilences, famines, earthquakes, the sea and the waves roaring, apostasy, immorality, race hatred, signs in the sky, flying saucers, earth satellites, violence in the atmosphere, cyclones, tornadoes and hurricanes without precedence, all these point unmistakably to that time of which Jesus said:

All these are the beginning of sorrows (Matt. 24:8).

Add to this the distinct human possibility of atomic annihilation (except for the restraining hand of God), and the universal preaching of the Gospel, and we have every reason to believe these are the foreboding shadows of the great Tribulation. It is the night of threshing and judgment of the nations. It is called "the day of the Lord." But the most significant sign of all is the recent return of the nation of Israel to the land of Palestine. It was toward the end of the harvest time that Naomi returned to Bethlehem and the winnowing night was at hand. Naomi is a picture of Israel, and Israel's return to her covenant land means that the next thing will be the dark night of earth's tribulation. Consider the words of the prophet Joel:

For, behold, in those days and in that time, when I shall bring again the captivity of Judah and Jerusalem (Joel 3:1).

Before going on to verse 2, note well the *time* about which Joel is speaking. He says "in those days," and we ask, "What days?" He says, "and in that time," and we inquire, "What time?" And the Holy Spirit answers through Joel —

When I shall bring again the captivity of Judah and Jerusalem (Joel 3:1).

Joel pinpoints the time of the fulfillment of his following prophecy. It will be *at that time* and *in those days,* when God shall bring again the captivity of Judah and Jerusalem. Surely none but the wilfully blind can miss *those days* and *that time.* They are *now!* In 1948 Judah returned as a nation from her captivity and established the State of Israel. Jerusalem was partially restored and the complete liberation of Jerusalem and the restoration of the whole of Canaan to the nation awaits only one event — the Wedding of Ruth and Boaz.

THE NATIONS PREPARING

Now what does Joel say will happen when the captivity of Judah is over? The words are plain (Joel 3):

I will also gather all nations, and bring them down into the valley of Jehoshaphat, and will plead with them there for my people and for my heritage Israel, whom they have scattered among the nations, and parted my land.

Proclaim ye this among the Gentiles; Prepare war, wake up the mighty men, let all the men of war draw near; let them come up:

Let the heathen be awakened, and come up to the valley of Jehoshaphat: for there will I sit to judge all the heathen round about.

Put ye in the sickle, for the harvest is ripe: come, get you down; for the press is full, the fats overflow; for their wickedness is great.

Multitudes, multitudes in the valley of decision: for the day of the LORD is near in the valley of decision.

The sun and the moon shall be darkened, and the stars shall withdraw their shining.

The LORD also shall roar out of Zion, and utter his voice

from Jerusalem; and the heavens and the earth shall shake: but the LORD will be the hope of his people, and the strength of the children of Israel (Joel 3:2, 9,12-16).

THE DAY OF THE LORD

This is God's description of the coming night of tribulation when according to Habakkuk God shall:

. . . march through the land in indignation . . . [and] . . . thresh the heathen in anger (Hab. 3:12).

It is God's threshing time, but when it comes, the Church, the bride, will be safe with her Lord and Master. During that night of threshing on Boaz' threshingfloor, Ruth was sweetly resting at Boaz' feet, while they talked and discussed their marriage, and made plans and prepared for the wedding to take place when the night was over. This too we see in Joel's prophecy when, after describing that awful time of trouble when the sun and the moon are darkened and the heavens and the earth shall shake, he adds this:

[*But*] the LORD will be the hope of his people, and the strength of the children of Israel (Joel 3:16b).

THE HOPE OF HIS PEOPLE

When this time comes, the Great Tribulation, believers will be with their Lord. The Lord will be the hope of His people as they rest in His blessed presence. The Blessed Hope of God's people is the coming of the Lord *before the tribulation.* We are looking — not for the tribulation — but we are:

Looking for that blessed hope, and the glorious appearing of the great God and our Saviour Jesus Christ (Titus 2:13).

But at that time God will also be the strength of the children of Israel. They will have to pass through this tribulation, but purified and saved, come out of it and as Joel continues:

> Judah shall dwell for ever, and Jerusalem from generation to generation (Joel 3:20).

While Ruth was resting at Boaz' feet, Naomi spent an anxious night in the darkness, but joy came to her in the morning.

Today the shadows of coming judgment are lengthening as the nations teeter on a powder keg. The time of reaping is almost over. The harvest is almost done and soon the night of judgment will fall upon a wicked world, and God shall thresh the nations, and for a long night of seven years judgment upon judgment, calamity upon calamity will fall upon the nations, until men shall seek to hide in hills and caves, calling for the rocks and the mountains to fall upon them and hide them from the face of Him who sitteth upon the throne and from the wrath of the Lamb.

But while all this is happening, the Church, the Bride of Christ, will be safe with her Lord. He has promised her:

> Because thou hast kept the word of my patience, I also will keep thee from the hour of temptation, which shall come upon all the world, to try them that dwell upon the earth (Rev. 3:10).

In closing let me ask, "Are you ready for that day, when you shall meet the Lord?" The darkness is deepening and soon it will be too late. The decision is yours. Ruth and her sister-in-law, Orpah, both faced the same decision. Ruth made the right choice. Orpah was left behind. Oh, heed today His invitation.

CHAPTER FOURTEEN

The Year of Jubilee

IT IS morning. The long night is past, and the rising sun dispels the gloom of night with its terror and fear. And it is in the morning the Gentile widow Ruth is to become the happy bride of the wealthy Jew of Bethlehem, Boaz. It is a glad, a joyous day for both Naomi and for Ruth as well as for Boaz. Naomi had returned from exile in Moab, but up until now had not received her lost inheritance. Ruth had been gleaning in the field but was still garbed in widow's clothes. But now comes the day when Naomi will receive her lost property again and Ruth will become Mrs. Boaz, and ancestor of the greater Boaz who was to be born in Bethlehem's stable 1300 years later. And so we come to the day of final redemption. Boaz had promised to marry Ruth and preparations had been made the night before. And now the marriage is to be legalized. We turn to Ruth 4:

> Then went Boaz up to the gate, and sat him down there. And he took ten men of the elders of the city, and said, Sit ye down here (Ruth 4:1, 2).

Here we see Boaz the Bethlehemite calling an assembly of the elders of the city to present himself in the role of a Redeemer. It is the clearest type of the Lord Jesus Christ as the Redeemer of His people to be found anywhere in the Scripture. It is rich beyond description and needs to be studied without haste, lest we miss its precious lessons.

105

MAN OF MANY NAMES

The name, Redeemer, as applied to Christ is not only a very common name in Scripture, but rich in meaning and full of instruction concerning God's plan of salvation. To truly appreciate the story of Ruth's redemption by Boaz we must understand the Scriptural meaning of the words, "redeem, redeemer and redemption." The word translated "redeem" in the Old Testament is "gaal" and means to "buy back," or to set free. It is the act whereby when, after a person's property or his liberty had been forfeited to another, it could be bought back again upon the payment of the legal price set by the law. Thus if one had lost title to a home or piece of land, the law made provision whereby at any time it could be bought back again. Today it may be compared to "pawning" one's property with the privilege of redeeming it later. This law also applied to a slave who had sold himself for debts or other obligations, but could be redeemed and set free. A third application of the law of redemption was for childless widows. If a husband died without leaving a child, then the husband's brother was to take his deceased brother's wife and raise up his name in Israel. This was the law of redemption of property, persons and widows.

ALL PRESENT IN RUTH

All these three aspects of redemption are found in the Book of Ruth. Naomi and Ruth had lost claim to the estate of Elimelech, through Naomi's absence and default. She had forfeited her claim to the family estate. This was subject to redemption. Ruth also had lost her liberty, for she was a Gentile outcast and outside the covenant blessing of Israel. This could only be redeemed, as she was accepted in the family of God's people by her marriage to Boaz. But she was also a widow, and needed a kinsman-redeemer.

REDEMPTION OF PROPERTY

We take up first the redemption of property. It is clearly outlined in detail in Leviticus 25:24, 25,

> And in all the land of your possession ye shall grant a redemption for the land.
> If thy brother be waxen poor, and hath sold away some of his possession, and if any of his kin come to redeem it, then shall he redeem that which his brother sold.

This provision was based upon the principle of divine ownership. No Israelite really ever owned any of the land, but was merely God's tenant. In Leviticus 25:23 God says:

> The land shall not be sold for ever, for the land is mine; for ye are strangers and sojourners with me.

The individual Israelite was merely God's tenant and, therefore, could not permanently dispose of the land. The nation as such held title, under God, to Canaan, but the rights of the individual were only temporary. No one could hold title to any property for more than fifty years. At the end of that time, during the year of Jubilee, all property reverted back to the original owner who held it at the previous year of Jubilee. A man, therefore, could not sell his property beyond the year of Jubilee which came at the end of seven sabbatic years. Every seventh year was a sabbatic year when the land was to rest. At the end of seven of these sabbatic years came this year of Jubilee. If a man bought a piece of property in the first year after the Jubilee he could hold it for 49 years. If he acquired it 20 years after the previous Jubilee, he could not hold it more than 29 years. If it was only five years before the next year of Jubilee, he must relinquish at the end of the five years. The price he was to pay would be on the basis of the years remaining till the next Jubilee.

Could Be Redeemed

If a person had acquired a piece of property from an unfortunate brother, because of his failure to pay a debt, then the property must be given back to the poor brother at the end of the seven sabbatic years. But now here comes the redemption clause. The law contained an important provision. At any time *before* the year of Jubilee that lost property could be bought back and redeemed. The law was clear on this and the price was to be determined by the number of years left until the fiftieth year. Here is the record:

The land shall not be sold for ever: for the land is mine; for ye are strangers and sojourners with me.

And in all the land of your possession ye shall grant a redemption for the land.

If thy brother be waxen poor, and hath sold away some of his possession, and if any of his kin come to redeem it, then shall he redeem that which his brother sold.

And if the man have none to redeem it, and himself be able to redeem it;

Then let him count the years of the sale thereof, and restore the overplus unto the man to whom he sold it; that he may return unto his possession.

But if he be not able to restore it to him, then that which is sold shall remain in the hand of him that hath bought it until the year of jubile: and in the jubile it shall go out, and he shall return unto his possession (Lev. 25:23-28).

Naomi's Lost Estate

This was exactly Naomi's sad condition upon her return to Bethlehem. The land which belonged to Elimelech, her deceased husband, had fallen into the hands of another. By abandoning her home and failing to meet her financial obligations, she had to forfeit her estate to a creditor. She was bankrupt, unable to do a thing to restore it. And now here the redeemer steps in. Boaz, a kinsman of Elimelech and Naomi, offers to redeem that lost inheritance by paying the debt for poor Naomi, and also Ruth as a legal heir by virtue of her marriage to Mahlon, the son of Naomi. But in order to be eligible as a redeemer of lost property, he must meet certain conditions. Not every person could act as redeemer. He must first of all be related to the person to be redeemed. By birth he must be a near kinsman. This too was definitely commanded.

> And if a sojourner or stranger wax rich by thee, and thy brother that dwelleth by him wax poor, and sell himself unto the stranger or sojourner by thee, or to the stock of the stranger's family:
> After that he is sold he may be redeemed again; one of his brethren may redeem him:
> Either his uncle, or his uncle's son, may redeem him, or any that is nigh of kin unto him of his family may redeem him; or if he be able, he may redeem himself.
> And he shall reckon with him that bought him from the year that he was sold to him unto the year of jubile: and the price of his sale shall be according unto the number of years, according to the time of an hired servant shall it be with him (Lev. 25:47-50).

But there was more. In addition to being a kinsman, the redeemer must also be willing to redeem, for it must be a voluntary act on the part of the redeemer. Then there was a third provision; the redeemer must be financially able to pay the redemption price. All three of these conditions Boaz was able to meet. He was related to the bankrupt one. In Ruth 2:1 we read:

> And Naomi had a kinsman of her husband's, a mighty man of wealth, of the family of Elimelech; and his name was Boaz.

Here are two of the three conditions fully met by Boaz. He was a kinsman and he was very wealthy. Only one question remained, Was he willing? This was settled the night of the winnowing when Boaz promised:

> I will do the part of a kinsman to thee (Ruth 3:13).

As concerning the redemption of Naomi's lost property, he was willing also and publicly declared his intentions in Ruth 4:3:

And he [Boaz] said unto the kinsman, Naomi, that is come again out of the country of Moab, selleth a parcel of land, which was our brother Elimelech's.

The verse is better translated "Naomi hath sold away a parcel of ground." She had lost it by default. And Boaz says to the other kinsman:

Buy it before the inhabitants, and before the elders of my people. If thou wilt redeem it, redeem it: but if thou wilt not redeem it, then tell me, that I may know (Ruth 4:4).

This nearer kinsman whom we shall identify later was unable to redeem it, and so Boaz declares:

Ye are witnesses this day, that I have bought [back] all that was Elimelech's, and all that was Chilion's and Mahlon's, of the hand of Naomi (Ruth 4:9).

ISRAEL'S REDEMPTION

We remind you again that Naomi is a picture of Israel, once planted in the land which God calls HIS land. They were tenants of Jehovah, but lost claim to their possession by their absence for centuries in the Moab of the Gentile nations. Then Israel returned and the land is to be restored to her again. Israel today has almost ended her wanderings in the Moab of her exile. She is as a nation back in the land, while the Church is gathering up the last gleanings of the harvest. Then will come earth's darkest night while the Church rests at the Redeemer's feet. It will be the night of tribulation, the "time of Jacob's trouble." And then the Redeemer will publicly appear like Boaz sitting in the gate, surrounded by the witnesses. He will redeem the land and restore it to Israel for ever and redeem them spiritually as well. This will usher in the year of Jubilee, when the exiles will return to their inheritance and know their Redeemer and Lord.

JUBILEE! JUBILEE!

How our hearts thrill as we read God's wonderful prophetic provision way back in Leviticus. Before we close we want to quote part of this chapter, and recommend it to you for your own careful study.

> And thou shalt number seven sabbaths of years unto thee, seven times seven years. . . .
> Then shalt thou cause the trumpet of the jubile to sound on the tenth day of the seventh month . . .
> And ye shall hallow the fiftieth year, and proclaim liberty throughout all the land unto all the inhabitants thereof: it shall be a jubile unto you; *and ye shall return every man unto his possession,* and ye shall return every man unto his family (Lev. 25:8-11).

The year of Israel's Jubilee is almost here. The harvest is ending, and soon the Church will be caught away and then after Israel's great trial, the year of Jubilee will come when — "Judah shall be saved, and Israel shall dwell safely." —

> And the land shall yield her fruit, and ye shall eat your fill, and dwell therein in safety (Lev. 25:19).

This is the law of the redemption of Israel's land. But there is another application for all of us. Man too was happy in perfect fellowship in the Garden of Eden. But sin drove him out, and he lost his inheritance. But God has provided a Redeemer, a Kinsman, the Lord Jesus, to redeem us and buy us back from the slave market of sin, and adopt us into the family of God, and make us heirs of God and joint heirs with Jesus Christ. Do you know Him? Soon He is coming, and then it will be too late. Receive Him *now*!

CHAPTER FIFTEEN

Sold Under Sin

And Naomi had a kinsman of her husband's, a mighty man
of wealth. . . . and his name was Boaz (Ruth 2:1).

NAOMI the widow of Elimelech had returned to Bethlehem
after almost ten years of exile, only to find the title to her
estate and home forfeited because of default during her
absence. Unless someone could be found to redeem it, she
must die in misery and poverty. But she had a kinsman, a
relative, who according to the law might redeem her lost
property. In our previous message we studied the law of
redemption as it related to the restoration of lost property.
According to the law, if a person were a close relative of
the bankrupt one, if he had the price of redemption, and if he
were willing, then he could buy back the lost estate. In
the case of Naomi this redeemer was Boaz, great type of our
Redeemer, Jesus. He met all these requirements. So too,
Israel's lost claim to the land of Canaan will be redeemed
by their coming Messiah, the greater than Boaz, the Lord
Jesus Christ.

A SERVANT REDEEMED

The law, however, had made provision for three things
which could be redeemed. In addition to redemption of real
estate, provision was also made for the redemption of a
servant or a slave, and for a widow whose husband died without leaving an issue. As to the redemption of a man's

liberty, the same provision was made as for the buying back of a lost estate. If a person unable to pay a debt had sold himself to his creditor until the debt should be paid, he could be set at liberty by being redeemed by a kinsman or a relative. Again this redeemer must be a close relative, he must be able to pay the redemption price, and he must be willing, for it must be a voluntary redemption.

We Too Were Slaves

All this, of course, was a type and a picture of our redemption by our Kinsman-Redeemer, the Lord Jesus. Of this Boaz was a type. He not only offered to redeem Naomi's inheritance, but also the lost position of Ruth. Ruth was a widow and a servant. Instead of a favored bride, she was a poverty-stricken gleaner, working in the field for a living. From this slavery and poverty Boaz was also willing to redeem her. In all this we see the fallen human race of Adam. Once, too, man was free and in perfect fellowship with his Creator and Maker. And then sin came in and man lost his freedom and became a slave to sin and toil and disease and death. For a mouthful of food from a forbidden tree, he relinquished his claim to liberty and life and became the subject of corruption and decay and must finally succumb to death. For a mess of pottage he sold his birthright and is hopelessly lost, unless redeemed by another.

In Romans 7, the apostle Paul describes in great detail the hopelessness of man under sin, and says:

> For I was alive without the law once: but when the commandment came, sin revived, and I died.
>
> And the commandment, which was ordained to life, I found to be unto death.
>
> For sin, taking occasion by the commandment, deceived me, and by it slew me.

Wherefore the law is holy, and the commandment holy, and just, and good.

For we know that the law is spiritual: but I am carnal, *sold under sin* (Romans 7:9-12, 14).

Sold Under Sin

According to the law we are guilty, condemned and lost, and as Paul says, *sold under sin.* We have sold ourselves, forfeited our life and liberty. Being dead in sin, there is nothing we can do to help ourselves. We can only cast ourselves upon the mercy of another. We need a Redeemer.

How beautifully this is illustrated in Ruth! Poor, lonely, toiling, widowed Ruth, could do nothing to redeem herself, but she could go to Boaz, the kinsman, and lay herself down at his feet, and hope for mercy. And she was not disappointed. So too, while we were utterly lost, God provided a Redeemer in the person of Christ, and we are invited to come to Him and find mercy and grace.

Redemption of a Widow

In addition to property and slavery, the law of redemption applied also to a widow whose husband died without leaving an issue to perpetuate the family name. It was considered a great tragedy in ancient times for a man to be childless and have no offspring so that his name ceased at his death. It was considered a sign of God's disfavor and judgment to be without children. Abraham complained bitterly because he had no heir. Isaac entreated God passionately for his wife Rebecca. Samuel's mother felt the sting of her barrenness and wept before the Lord while entreating for a child. Tradition tells us that every godly woman in Israel greatly desired children in the hope that one of them would be in the line of ancestry of their promised Messiah — Redeemer.

GOD'S GREAT PROVISION

To meet this situation, if a man died before he had begotten children, God gave some definite instructions in Deuteronomy 25:5, 6,

> If brethren dwell together, and one of them die, and have no child, the wife of the dead shall not marry without unto a stranger: her husband's brother shall go in unto her, and take her to him to wife, and perform the duty of an husband's brother unto her.
>
> And it shall be, that the firstborn which she beareth shall succeed in the name of his brother which is dead, that his name be not put out of Israel.

This was the law which the Sadducees referred to when they came to Jesus in Matthew 22. They came to Jesus and said:

> Master, Moses said, If a man die, having no children, his brother shall marry his wife, and raise up seed unto his brother.
>
> Now there were with us seven brethren: and the first, when he had married a wife, deceased, and, having no issue, left his wife unto his brother.
>
> Likewise the second also, and the third, unto the seventh.
> And last of all the woman died also (Matt. 22:24-26).

From this it seems evident that the law was still considered valid and was being observed in the time of Christ. Naomi also referred to this law when she appealed to Orpha and Ruth to return to their people. She said:

> Turn again, my daughters: Why will ye go with me? Are there yet any more sons in my womb, that they may be your husbands? (Ruth 1:11)

But when Naomi came to Bethlehem she found that there were at least two kinsmen who were related closely enough to be eligible to legally marry Ruth.

THE SHAME OF FAILURE

Boaz was a kinsman, to be sure, but there was another relative of Naomi who was more closely related than Boaz, and he must be given the first opportunity. And so in order to settle this matter Boaz calls a city council meeting to determine the matter. In the morning after his interview with Ruth on the threshingfloor, Boaz immediately proceeds to settle this important matter.

> Then went Boaz up to the gate, and sat him down there: and, behold, the kinsman of whom Boaz spake came by; unto whom he said, Ho, such a one! turn aside, sit down here. And he turned aside, and sat down.
> And he took ten men of the elders of the city, and said, Sit ye down here. And they sat down (Ruth 4:1,2).

PORTRAIT OF BOAZ

In these two verses we learn some wonderful things about Boaz. First he evidently was a man with unusual authority. The gate of the city was the place where the elders sat in council session to hear and judge matters of dispute, and render decisions concerning legal matters. Boaz seems to have been the head of the group. He probably was the mayor of the city. He had great power and influence and he spoke with a voice of authority. When he said to the kinsman, "Ho, such a one!" or as it might be translated, "Ho, you over there, sit down here," immediately the man sat down. Then he orders ten men of the elders, councilmen, if you please, and says, "Sit down here," and they sat down. The word of Boaz seemed to be final.

In addition to being a mighty man with authority, and respected by all, he was a *just man*. This matter must be settled *legally*. Boaz was in love with Ruth and with his great position of power, authority and wealth, could have ignored the claim of his kinsman rival, and just married Ruth. But no — this thing must meet the demands of the law, and to further make it legal, he calls a council of ten men of the elders of the city. Ten members constituted a quorum, and was the number of complete testimony. Every single letter of the law is met. There was another kinsman who had a claim on Ruth's hand and a responsibility to Naomi in the redemption of her property. He must be heard and his claim given full recognition.

And thirdly, notice this was not done in a corner, but was made a public transaction. When Boaz paid out the money for the redemption of Naomi's property, and when he took Ruth and redeemed her, it was before the eyes of all the inhabitants of the city.

Picture of Our Saviour

All of this becomes a wonderful picture of our great Redeemer, the Lord Jesus, whom Boaz so beautifully foreshadows. He too met all the conditions of the law which testified against us. He led a perfect, sinless life for thirty-three years and thereby satisfied the law in his own life and provided a perfect righteousness for us. Then at the end of His ministry, He went to the Cross and there paid the debt of a broken law for us. He, like Boaz, was mighty and able, fit and willing, and made full satisfaction to the broken law by paying the price of eternal separation from God.

Because He was infinite God, He could in a moment of time pay the infinite price of redemption for our sin. And when He said, "It is finished," every single legal claim of the law had been met, the last farthing had been paid, and He received the receipt, "Paid in full," from the hand of God, when He raised Him from the dead. Had one single sin remained unatoned, He could not have arisen, for the wages of sin (one single sin) is death.

Moreover, it was a public transaction. Our Redeemer, when He died to pay our debt, was not executed in a cell, or a death chamber, but out in the open for all to see. It was in addition on a *hill*, and added to this, on a *tree*. Out in the open, on a hill, and on a tree! Everyone was able to see it. None were barred from the scene, no matter how far removed. He Himself had said in John 3:

> And as Moses lifted up the serpent in the wilderness, even so must the Son of man be lifted up:
> That whosoever believeth in him should not perish, but have eternal life (John 3:14, 15).

In John 8:28 Jesus said:

> When ye have lifted up the Son of man, then shall ye know that I am he.

And again in John 12:32 Jesus said:

> And I, if I be lifted up from the earth, will draw all men unto me.

Today you have once more seen the uplifted Redeemer, dying to save you if you will but believe. There is no more excuse for you, for you cannot plead ignorance anymore. You have seen Him on the Cross, lifted up before all, towering above all else, and now it is up to you, like Ruth the Moabitess, to make your decision.

CHAPTER SIXTEEN

What the Law Could Not Do

An Ammonite or Moabite shall not enter into the congregation of the LORD (Deut. 23:3).

THE widow, Ruth, was a Moabite, a stranger to the covenants of promise made to Israel. The law barred the way, but by a marvelous plan of redemption she was able to take her place not only in Israel, but even in the royal line of ancestors of the coming Redeemer. The Book of Ruth is preeminently a book of redemption. While we have placed great emphasis on the dispensational and prophetic aspect of the book, we cannot dissociate this from the subject of redemption. All of this is an illustration of our redemption. Ruth was a penniless widow, and like Naomi, powerless to redeem herself. The law demanded a price of redemption, and failure to furnish the legal payment left her hopeless. The law could not help her. But another comes and meets the conditions required by the law, and fully redeems the poor, lost widow. We too like Ruth, stand condemned before the perfect law of God.

THE POWERLESS LAW

The law is totally powerless to justify, save, or redeem the sinner. The law knows only justice. Its demands are absolute, it can show no mercy to the transgressor. But here God enters in with His wonderful message of grace. The law could not save, justify, or sanctify the sinner. It cannot make

119

the sinner a saint, it cannot forgive sin, it cannot change the heart, it cannot teach us to live better, it cannot help us out of our predicament in any way whatsoever. All the law can do is demand punishment and justice, and pronounce our sentence, reveal our filthiness and unworthiness, and curse us with eternal death. That is the sole ministry of the law. It was never intended to save. God knew when He gave the law it would never save a single sinner, never make a single man better. He knew that no sinner would ever keep it. Yea, more than that, God knew that the very people He commanded to keep that law—could not in themselves keep it at all. This was not the fault of the law. It established the absolute justice and righteousness of the law. It was the fault of the flesh. Paul says in Romans 8:3:

> For what the law COULD NOT DO, in that it was weak through the flesh. . . .

Will you please notice the first phrase of that verse! "For what the law COULD NOT DO!" There are some things then the law cannot do, and God never expected it to do. We ask, therefore, what was it? It could not justify; it could not save, or pardon, or redeem, or improve, or fix up, or help, or assist, forgive, or change the heart of the sinner. Now this is not a fault or any weakness of the law, but because of the strength of the law, and the weakness of the human flesh and heart. And so Paul adds after he says, "For what the law could not do, IN THAT IT WAS WEAK THROUGH THE FLESH." It was the weakness of the flesh which prevented the law from doing anything but cursing the sinner. The sinner's flesh is so corrupt, even the saint's flesh is so filthy and corrupt, and because the law is so holy and perfect and just, it can only condemn such who have not kept the law.

What Then Is Our Hope?

But now comes a glorious revelation. What the law COULD NOT DO, the Lord Jesus Christ DID DO. He came to deliver us from the curse of the law. Yes, Jesus came to deliver us from the law itself. The law was a slave driver, an executioner, seeking to kill us because of our sins. Then Jesus comes and does two things: first, He lives a perfect, holy, sinless life for thirty-three and one-half years in full and complete obedience to the law of God in every detail. He thereby provided a righteousness, a positive righteousness of the law. Then He did the second thing; He paid the death penalty of the law when He died on Calvary and proved that He had paid it all by rising from the grave after three days. The penalty of the law was paid at Calvary, and thereby He has provided a perfect righteousness by His sinless life which is imputed to those who believe on Him. Now the Lord Jesus Christ offers both of these by faith through grace to any sinner who will turn from the law to Him—from his works to Christ—and be saved. To every sinner who will admit that he could not keep the law of God and will receive the Lord Jesus Christ, He does two things.

First, He imputes His death and resurrection to that sinner. The law is satisfied in Christ, it has exacted its full penalty in Him, and this righteousness is accounted to the sinner. He now is a redeemed sinner whose debt has been fully paid.

Second, Jesus imputes to this forgiven sinner His perfect righteousness which He proved and provided by His own sinless life, in perfect harmony with the law; and now the believing sinner is clothed with the righteousness of Christ Himself. By the death of the Lord Jesus the believer has paid the penalty of the law which he owed. By the life of the Lord Jesus Christ he is now clothed with the perfect, sinless righteousness of Christ Himself, and stands before

God as though he had never committed a single sin in all his life and had never even once broken the holy law of God. That, my friend, is justification, a truth which few seem to understand. The saint is not a pardoned sinner, for the law knows no pardon. It knows only punishment, and that is what Paul says in Romans 8:

> For what the law could not do, in that it was weak through the flesh, God sending his own Son in the likeness of sinful flesh, and for sin, condemned sin in the flesh:
> That the righteousness of the law might be fulfilled in us, who walk not after the flesh, but after the Spirit (Rom. 8:3, 4).

Will you please notice that statement, "That the righteousness of the law might be fulfilled in us"? It does not say that the righteousness of the law might be fulfilled BY us, but rather, IN us. And the Lord Jesus Christ does that. The righteousness of the law to which we could not attain is provided by Him who bore our sins on Calvary in our stead. And so, turning to Galatians 3:10, we remind you of Paul's words:

> For as many as are of the works of the law are under the curse: for it is written, Cursed is every one that continueth not in all things which are written in the book of the law to do them.

That is what the law demanded! Hopeless, helpless, condemned, vile, filthy, guilty before God we stand, but what the law could not do, Jesus did, and so we read in Galatians 3:13,

> Christ hath redeemed us from the curse of the law, being made a curse for us: for it is written, Cursed is every one that hangeth on a tree.

UNDER THE LAW

And now we are delivered, we have been discharged forever from the law (Rom. 7:6). The law cannot condemn twice. The believer then is through with the law forever. He is delivered from the law, he is dead to the law (Gal. 2:19), and free from the law (Rom. 8:2). Oh, Christian, rejoice in this wonderful salvation and this marvelous redemption provided by the Lord Jesus Christ. May I repeat again:

> Cursed is every one that continueth not in all things which are written in the book of the law to do them.

It is not a matter of keeping the law partly, it is not a matter of living a holy life for a short time, but the Scripture says, "Cursed is every one that continueth not." It must be an uninterrupted, unbroken obedience to the law of God if we ever hope to find salvation by our own efforts and by our own works.

I do want to bring a definite appeal to those of you who are still without the Lord Jesus Christ, and are hoping to attain heaven and salvation without coming and believing on Him as your own personal Saviour. There are so many today who believe that if they live a good life and join a church and go through all the rituals of religion, and behave themselves, and make an honest effort to keep the law to the best of their ability, that then God will save them. The Bible knows nothing of this kind of a salvation. God says, "There is none that doeth good, no, not one." We have all gone astray, we are altogether become unprofitable. And for this very reason the Lord Jesus Christ had to die on the Cross of Calvary to provide that which we ourselves were absolutely unable to attain. The law is not intended to save, but rather to show us our need of salvation. It is, according to Paul, a schoolmaster, to teach us the lesson of our inability and to make us ready to receive the free gift of God by His own wonderful grace. Someone has compared the law to a mirror, in which we can see how soiled our face is, but which has no power to cleanse, and so we turn from the mirror after we have seen the awful condition of our own filthiness, and cast ourselves on Him who alone by His own precious blood can redeem us and wash us from our sins. And then, when we have received Him, God gives us the assurance that the law has been fulfilled by Christ. This righteousness is imputed to us, the penalty that He paid is now our payment of sin, and we can say:

> Free from the law, O happy condition,
> Jesus hath bled, and there is remission;
> Cursed by the law and bruised by the fall,
> Grace hath redeemed us once for all.
>
> Once for all, O sinner, receive it,
> Once for all, O brother, believe it;
> Cling to the Cross, the burden will fall,
> Christ hath redeemed us once for all.

CHAPTER SEVENTEEN

The Kinsman-Redeemer

IT was a law in Israel that in the event of a man's death, leaving a wife without children, the brother of the husband, providing he was able, was to take the widow of his brother to wife and raise up a seed in the stead of his deceased brother. In the event that such a kinsman-redeemer failed to carry out the provisions of this law, he was to be publicly disgraced and pay an awful penalty. After stating this law of a widow's redemption in Deuteronomy 25:5, 6, the record continues:

> And if the man like not to take his brother's wife, then let his brother's wife go up to the gate unto the elders, and say, My husband's brother refuseth to raise up unto his brother a name in Israel, he will not perform the duty of my husband's brother.
>
> Then the elders of his city shall call him, and speak unto him: and if he stand to it, and say, I like not to take her;
>
> Then shall his brother's wife come unto him in the presence of the elders, and loose his shoe from off his foot, and spit in his face, and shall answer and say, So shall it be done unto that man that will not build up his brother's house.
>
> And his name shall be called in Israel, The house of him that hath his shoe loosed (Deut. 25:7-10).

A striking illustration of the application of this law is found in the Book of Ruth. Her husband, Mahlon, had died in Moab. There was a kinsman of Ruth's husband, whose name is not given, who would bear the first obligation of taking Ruth as his wife. Before Boaz, therefore, could lay claim to Ruth's hand, this nearer relative must be heard. And Boaz informs Ruth of this in Ruth 3:12, 13,

> And now it is true that I am thy near kinsman: howbeit there is a kinsman nearer than I.
>
> Tarry this night, and it shall be in the morning, that if he will perform unto thee the part of a kinsman, well; let him do the kinsman's part: but if he will not do the part of a kinsman to thee, then will I do the part of a kinsman to thee, as the Lord liveth: lie down until the morning (Ruth 3:12, 13).

This kinsman must be given the first opportunity, but as chapter four relates, he was unable to meet all of the three conditions. Here is the conversation as we have it in Ruth, chapter 4:

> Then went Boaz up to the gate, and sat him down there: and, behold, the kinsman of whom Boaz spake came by; unto whom he said, Ho, such a one! turn aside, sit down here. And he turned aside, and sat down.
>
> And he took ten men of the elders of the city, and said, Sit ye down here. And they sat down.
>
> And he said unto the kinsman, Naomi, that is come again out of the country of Moab, selleth a parcel of land, which was our brother Elimelech's:
>
> And I thought to advertise thee, saying, Buy it before the inhabitants, and before the elders of my people. If thou wilt redeem it, redeem it: but if thou wilt not redeem it, then tell me, that I may know: for there is none to redeem it beside thee; and I am after thee. And he said, I will redeem it (Ruth 4:1-4).

This kinsman, you will notice from this conversation, was perfectly willing to act as a redeemer. He would very much like to, but there was one obstacle which stood in the way, for he must meet three conditions. And so we find Boaz saying in verses 5 and 6:

> Then said Boaz, What day thou buyest the field of the hand of Naomi, thou must buy it also of Ruth the Moabitess,

the wife of the dead, to raise up the name of the dead upon his inheritance.

And the kinsman said, I cannot redeem it for myself, lest I mar mine own inheritance: redeem thou my right to thyself; for I cannot redeem it (Ruth 4:5,6).

THE SHAME OF WEAKNESS

In Israel it was considered a great disgrace for anyone to refuse or be unable to redeem his unfortunate brother. A very solemn and humiliating ritual was, therefore, publicly held to proclaim to all men that a kinsman had been unable to redeem those who depended upon him. In this fourth chapter of Ruth, and verse 7, we have mention made of the law concerning this kinsman-redeemership.

Now this was the manner in former time in Israel concerning redeeming and concerning changing, for to confirm all things; a man plucked off his shoe, and gave it to his neighbour: and this was a testimony in Israel.

Therefore the kinsman said unto Boaz, Buy it for thee. So he drew off his shoe (Ruth 4:7, 8).

This left only Boaz who could now act as the redeemer without a rival. Before looking at the solemn ritual which follows, we must of necessity try to answer some questions concerning this nearer kinsman who failed in the role of redeemer even though he was closer to Ruth than Boaz. There have been various interpretations, but the most common one is, that while Boaz typifies the Lord Jesus, this other nearer relative represents the law. This is the almost universal interpretation. We are told that this redeemer who was unable to buy back Naomi's inheritance or redeem Ruth's widowhood was the law of commandments. The ten elders are taken to mean the Ten Commandments written on stone. The curse of the law rested upon Ruth who was a Moabite, and the law had said, "An Ammonite or Moabite shall not enter into the congregation of the Lord." Therefore, the law could not bring Ruth into the family of Elimelech, but could only keep her out, and under the curse.

However, this interpretation fails to fit the picture in several points. It is an application, and as such we have no objection to it, but as an interpretation, it fails to satisfy. Boaz was A PERSON, and therefore, the near kinsman must also be a person. We believe there is a nearer relative who fully meets all the conditions. Certainly it was no fault of the law that it could not redeem us. The fault was ours, and not the law, for the law is holy and perfect and righteous and just. To say that the nearer kinsman is the law is to accuse God of giving an imperfect law. The blame lies entirely with the sinner. Paul tells us in Romans:

> For what the law could not do, in that it was weak through the flesh, God sending his own Son in the likeness of sinful flesh, and for sin, condemned sin in the flesh:
>
> That the righteousness of the law might be fulfilled in us, who walk not after the flesh, but after the Spirit (Rom. 8: 3, 4).

The trouble was with the flesh, not the law. A holy law could not justify the sinner. And so we must look for someone else besides the law to be our nearer kinsman.

WHO THEN IS HE?

Who is a nearer kinsman than Jesus to us? Who is more closely related to mankind than Jesus? The answer is, our own fellow-brothers in the flesh are in a sense nearer even than Christ was. All of Adam's children are nearer kinsman, but all are sinners and cannot even redeem themselves. In Adam you are my kinsman, and I am yours. No man can by any means redeem his brother. See how clearly it is stated here in Ruth, chapter 4, and verse 6:

> And the kinsman said, I cannot redeem it for myself, lest I mar mine own inheritance: redeem thou my right to thyself; for I cannot redeem it.

The kinsman had a debt of his own to pay. How then could he pay for another? Unable to pay our own debt, how can we hope to be another's redeemer? What a picture all of this becomes of us! No matter how much we would like to save and redeem others, our own loved ones, and nearest relatives, our wives and children, we cannot, for we are unable to redeem ourselves. We can meet the two first requirements, but the third is impossible. We are fit, to be sure, as far as being related by human nature is concerned, and many of us, like this kinsman in Ruth, are willing, but we are wholly unable. We ourselves need a redeemer. How then shall we be able to redeem ourselves?

To pay the debt of another, we must be free of debt ourselves. If we cannot even pay for our own sin, then how can we hope to pay for another's? It is not possible for a sinner to amass sufficient righteousness for himself to satisfy the just demands of God's law; how then can he have enough works over and above his own requirements which can be applied to another who is deficient in his own right? Ah, no, beloved, there is no such thing as transferring our good deeds, our works, our righteousness to another, when we ourselves are wholly bankrupt and lost. David declares in Psalm 14:

> The Lord looked down from heaven upon the children of men, to see if there were any that did understand, and seek God.
> They are all gone aside, they are all together become filthy: there is none that doeth good, no, not one (Ps. 14:2, 3).

Even after we are saved, we cannot redeem another, for all the righteousness we then possess is *His* righteousness, and not our own. The nearer kinsman than Boaz must, therefore, represent the natural seed of Adam. David says of man, no matter how powerful and wealthy he may be, that he is totally helpless to redeem another.

> They that trust in their wealth, and boast themselves in the multitude of their riches;
> None of them can by any means redeem his brother, nor give to God a ransom for him:
> [For the redemption of their soul is precious, and it ceaseth for ever] (Ps. 49:6-8).

And so, unless someone can be found who has no debt of his own to pay, we must be forever lost. But God found a way. He had a Son whom He sent to become a man, related to us by human birth, born of a human mother as we are; and so in our story Boaz enters the picture, after it has been proven man is totally powerless to save himself. The nearer kinsman has failed completely.

ENTER BOAZ

This being settled, there is none other left but Boaz, and he is fit and willing and able. What a humiliating lesson! So hopeless is our condition through sin that nothing less than Omnipotence can save us. So great is our own debt that nothing but the precious price of the blood of God's Son, the Lord Jesus Christ, is able to redeem us, and at what a cost this was done! First, He had to lay aside His glory in heaven, lay aside the form of God, and clothe Himself in humanity by His incarnation, so that He might be a kinsman to all of us. But that was not all. He must also provide the price. And so at the close of those thirty-three years of His ministry here, during which, as the Son of Man, the human Jesus, He identified Himself with all of humanity's problems, He prepared Himself to pay the price.

During those thirty-three years He experienced every trial and sorrow and problem and temptation to which mankind is subject and heir. Listen to Hebrews 4:15:

> For we have not an high priest which cannot be touched with the feeling of our infirmities; but was in all points tempted like as we are, yet without sin.

Or listen to Hebrews 2, verses 17 and 18:

> Wherefore in all things it behoved him to be made like unto his brethren, that he might be a merciful and faithful high priest in things pertaining to God, to make reconciliation for the sins of the people.
> For in that he himself hath suffered being tempted, he is able to succour them that are tempted.

So closely did the Lord Jesus Christ, our Redeemer, identify Himself with those whom He came to save, that He not only took on Him human nature, but human temptation and suffering and trial. He is indeed the Kinsman-Redeemer, but He must also be able; and so at the end of His life He went to Gethsemane where God laid upon Him our sin and our debt, and He took it, like Boaz, outside the gate, among many witnesses, and there weighed out the purchase price of redemption by His own precious, incorruptible and eternal blood, and some day will return to take us unto Himself as His precious, redeemed and blood-bought Bride.

CHAPTER EIGHTEEN

Take Off Your Shoes

Now this was the manner in former time in Israel concerning redeeming and concerning changing, for to confirm all things; a man plucked off his shoe, and gave it to his neighbour: and this was a testimony in Israel.

Therefore the kinsman said unto Boaz, Buy it for thee. So he drew off his shoe (Ruth 4:7, 8).

THE ritual by which a man, unable to redeem his brother, relinquished all claim to another was a dramatic and colorful ceremony. It was the duty of a near relative or kinsman to redeem the lost property or position of an impoverished brother. In the event he was unable to do so, he was submitted to a very disgraceful treatment. His fellows were to draw off his shoe and to spit in his face.

In Deuteronomy 25 we have this law given by Moses. If a brother of a deceased husband was unable to take his brother's widow to wife, he was submitted to the following disgraceful treatment:

Then shall his brother's wife come unto him in the presence of the elders, and loose his shoe from off his foot, and spit in his face, and shall answer and say, So shall it be done unto that man that will not build up his brother's house.

And his name shall be called in Israel, The house of him that hath his shoe loosed (Deut. 25:9, 10).

This procedure was followed in the Book of Ruth. Boaz had offered to redeem the lost possession of Naomi and the widowhood of Ruth, on one condition. This condition was the inability or unwillingness of a nearer relative than Boaz to undertake the redemption. And so Boaz sits in the gate, calls a council of ten elders, hails the nearer kinsman before him, and presents the case.

> And he said unto the kinsman, Naomi, that is come again out of the country of Moab, selleth a parcel of land [literally, has sold by default her land] which was our brother Elimelech's:
>
> And I thought to advertise thee, saying, Buy it before the inhabitants, and before the elders of my people. If thou wilt redeem it, redeem it: but if thou wilt not redeem it, then tell me, that I may know: for there is none to redeem it beside thee; and I am after thee. And he said, I will redeem it (Ruth 4: 3, 4).

Boaz offers this relative the first opportunity to redeem the lost property of Naomi, and he accepts. He is perfectly willing to do so. And then Boaz adds another provision, and says:

> What day thou buyest the field of the hand of Naomi, [literally, for Naomi] thou must buy it also of Ruth the Moabitess, the wife of the dead, to raise up the name of the dead upon his inheritance.
>
> And the kinsman said, I cannot redeem it for myself, lest I mar mine own inheritance: redeem thou my right to thyself; for I cannot redeem it (Ruth 4:5, 6).

This opened the way for Boaz to become the legal redeemer. Why the kinsman was unable to redeem the inheritance is not specifically stated, except that doing so would mar his own inheritance. Rabbinical tradition says that the kinsman was himself married and had two children. Another explanation is that the kinsman could redeem Naomi's share but not the portion of Ruth's inheritance by virtue of her marriage to Mahlon. But whatever the reason, he could not meet the conditions and so relinquished all claims as a redeemer to Boaz.

THE BAREFOOT MAN

Then follows the dramatic ritual of the taking off the shoe. It was an admission of failure, a severe rebuke for his inability to be the redeemer. He now must go about barefooted. The shoe is taken off, and handed to Boaz. The name of this nearer kinsman is not given, so he may well go by the name of Mr. Barefoot. Boaz had addressed him as "Ho, such a one." He is to become the barefooted kinsman as a stigma of unfaithfulness.

What a humiliation for this man! And remember this kinsman is a picture of everyone of us. No matter how willing we may be to redeem our loved ones, we are totally powerless to do so. We have another picture of this same thing in the history of Moses, who was the very one whom God used to write down this law of the unfaithful brother. We have the record of this in the story of the burning bush on the back side of the desert. You will recall, Moses had fled from his people Israel in Egypt, and sought safety in the desert for forty years. Now Moses was the kinsman-redeemer of the nation of Israel. He knew that he was to be the kinsman-redeemer, for we read very clearly in the address of Stephen before the Sanhedrin in Acts 7, concerning Moses:

> And when he was full forty years old, it came into his heart to visit his brethren the children of Israel.
> And seeing one of them suffer wrong, he defended him, and avenged him that was oppressed, and smote the Egyptian:
> For he supposed his brethren would have understood how that God by his hand would deliver them: but they understood not (Acts 7:23-25).

Moses was fit to be their redeemer, for he was one of their brethren; he was able, for he had been called of God and schooled for his task for forty years in the university of Egypt; but he was unwilling to redeem his brethren after their rejection of him, and so God meets him and brands him as one who failed to redeem his brethren. This was done by taking off the shoe from the unfaithful brother's foot, and God did just this, and God caused him to take off his shoe. Here is Stephen's record in Acts 7, beginning at verse 30:

> And when forty years were expired, there appeared to him in the wilderness of mount Sina an angel of the Lord in a flame of fire in a bush.
>
> When Moses saw it, he wondered at the sight: and as he drew near to behold it, the voice of the Lord came unto him,
>
> Saying, I am the God of thy fathers, the God of Abraham, and the God of Isaac, and the God of Jacob. Then Moses trembled, and durst not behold.
>
> Then said the Lord to him, Put off thy shoes from thy feet: for the place where thou standest is holy ground (Acts 7:30-33).

Moses had run away from his duty and had failed in his responsibility to his brethren in Egypt. That this is the meaning of the "loosing" of the shoe is evident from God's Word to Moses in Exodus 2. While Moses was trying to forget his mission, we read:

> And God heard their groaning, and God remembered his covenant with Abraham, with Isaac, and with Jacob.
>
> And God looked upon the children of Israel, and God had respect unto them (Ex. 2:24, 25).

And again when God meets Moses at the bush and after his shoes have been removed, God says to him:

> I have surely seen the affliction of my people which are in Egypt, and have heard their cry by reason of their taskmasters; for I know their sorrows;
>
> And I am come down to deliver them. . . .
>
> Come now therefore, and I will send thee unto Pharaoh, that thou mayest bring forth my people the children of Israel out of Egypt (Ex. 3:7, 8, 10).

JESUS ACCUSED ALSO

This also will throw light on the treatment afforded our Redeemer, the Lord Jesus Christ, when He stood in the judgment hall as our Saviour. Those who delivered Jesus and put Him to death considered Him as an imposter and one who had failed in His duty toward His brethren. When He came they expected Him to be their Redeemer and Deliverer. They looked for Him to declare Himself as King, and throw off the yoke of Roman oppression, and restore their liberty to them. In this expectation the crowds had followed Him, and thronged about Him. They had even tried to take Him by violence to make Him King. And now their hopes are shattered, His popularity wanes, and here He stands a helpless prisoner of the law, unable (as they supposed) to redeem His people. In order to emphasize their disappointment and heap disgrace upon Him, they resorted to the custom of spitting upon Him as an expression of utter disrespect for His failure. No less than six times it is recorded in the Gospels that they "spit" upon the Redeemer. In the light of the meaning of this act in Deuteronomy 25 and Ruth 4, the implication was clear. It was their way of saying, "He claimed to have come to redeem us, and He has utterly failed." Little did they know that He was taking our place, bearing our shame and reproach, and by His very rejection securing our redemption. And so we read in Matthew 26:

> Then did they spit in his face, and buffeted him; and others smote him with the palms of their hands,
> Saying, Prophesy unto us, thou Christ, Who is he that smote thee (Matt. 26:67, 68).

What ignominy, what shame He bore for us! They spit in His face and slapped Him with open hands in insult. They did not strike with the fist as one would a strong man, but slapped Him instead like a child or a woman. They implied He was a weakling who could not bear the blow of a fist, but must be slapped like a "sissy" and a weakling.

This first spitting was before the religious body of the Sanhedrin with Caiaphas presiding. But Matthew tells us it was repeated before the civil authorities with Pilate in the judgment hall. In Matthew 27:28 they strip Him. Presumably they took off His shoes, and then in verse 30:

> They spit upon him, and took the reed, and smote him on the head (Matt. 27:30).

The humiliation intensifies. For the second time they spit upon Him and then took a reed to strike Him over the head. Don't miss the implication here. They did not strike Him with a club or a stick, but with a *reed* — a soft, pliable, limp stalk of marsh grass, which Jesus said was shaken by the wind. What insult! He was such a weakling they would not even allow Him the dignity of being smitten by anything more than a frail, light, wind-blown reed.

Isaiah had prophesied all this centuries before when he cried:

> I gave my back to the smiters, and my cheeks to them that plucked off the hair: I hid not my face from shame and spitting (Isa. 50:6).

Isaiah adds still more disgraceful treatment. He says they "plucked off the hair," meaning they pulled out His beard, as if to say, "Why, He is not man enough to have a beard," and proceeded to pluck it out.

The evangelist, Mark, mentions the spitting no less than three times (Mark 10:34; 14:65; and 15:19). Little did His murderers know that He was bearing all this for them and in their place. This was all part of the price of their redemption. They themselves, and we ourselves, are the unworthy ones, who were unable to redeem.

Before closing this chapter we must return for a moment to the story of Ruth and Boaz. The kinsman had admitted his inability to meet the conditions of redemption, so the shoe is taken off and Mr. Barefoot relinquishes all claim to the redemptive process. The shoe is handed to Boaz, who accepts it. It is both an admission of failure and becomes for Boaz his marriage license. It is his certificate that he can now take Ruth to be his wife, having met every condition of the law. Surely one sees the lesson here for us. We are the nearer kinsman, disgraced and helpless. We too must relinquish all claim to our own redemption, and admit that only our Boaz, our Redeemer, the Lord Jesus, has the right, the power and the ability to save. Until we are willing to admit our total and complete inability to lift one finger toward our salvation, so long there can be no redemption. We must come to the place where we say:

> Not the labors of my hands,
>   Can fulfill Thy law's demands;
> Could my zeal no respite know,
>   Could my tears forever flow,
> These for sin could not atone;
>   Thou must save, and thou alone.
> Nothing in my hand I bring,
>   Simply to Thy cross I cling.

CHAPTER NINETEEN

The Incarnation of Christ

THE law which God gave to Israel by the hand of Moses demanded perfect and uninterrupted obedience. If this were the only provision God gave to Israel, they would all have been lost, for no man is able to keep the law of God perfectly and earn his salvation by obedience to this law. And so God gave, in addition to the law which slew and condemned the sinner, a plan of redemption whereby the law-breaker could receive mercy and be redeemed again. This was all foreshadowed in the provision God made whereby a slave could be set free and redeemed. In Leviticus 25 Moses declared:

> And if a sojourner or stranger wax rich by thee, and thy brother that dwelleth by him wax poor, and sell himself unto the stranger or sojourner by thee, or to the stock of the stranger's family:
>
> After that he is sold he may be redeemed again; one of his brethren may redeem him:
>
> Either his uncle, or his uncle's son, may redeem him, or any that is nigh of kin unto him of his family may redeem him; or if he be able, he may redeem himself (Lev. 25:47-49).

This law applied not only to personal liberty but personal property as well. And finally the law of redemption applied to a widow whose dead husband left her without an issue. Then a brother or kinsman of the deceased was to marry the widow. This law we have seen was followed in the case of Ruth the Moabitess, who was redeemed by Boaz the near kinsman.

139

Our Kinsman — Redeemer

All of this was, of course, typical of the Lord Jesus our Redeemer. This kinsman-redeemer, however, must meet three inviolable conditions. According to the law of redemption he must be:

1. A close relative — a member of the family of the one to be redeemed.

2. He must be able to pay the required price of the redemption.

3. He must be willing to be the redeemer — it must be a voluntary act.

In the case of the first and nearest kinsman in Ruth, he was willing and he was fitted by being related, but he failed because he was not able to pay the price. This is the case with us, who are the "nearer" kinsman. We too belong to the family of fallen humanity, thereby meeting the first requirement. We too may be ever so willing to redeem our loved ones, thereby meeting the third requirement. But when it comes to our ability to pay the price of their redemption, we fail completely.

Boaz and Christ

But there is one who is able to meet all three conditions. In the story of Ruth, Boaz was related, was able, and willing. How clear the Word is on this. As to Boaz meeting the first requirement, we read, "Now Naomi had a kinsman of her husband's." This took care of the first condition — he belonged to the family.

The second condition is taken care of by the next phrase, "a mighty man of wealth." He was able to meet the price demanded to redeem the inheritance of these poor widows. He was a mighty man of wealth. Then he met the third requirement, when he twice stated his willingness to marry poor Ruth. Once he states it in private on the night of their betrothal (Ruth

3:13), and then he makes the public declaration in chapter 4, verse 10,

> Moreover Ruth the Moabitess, the wife of Mahlon, have I purchased to be my wife . . . ye are witnesses this day (Ruth 4:10).

Boaz, the mighty man of Bethlehem, is one of the clearest and most beautiful types of our Redeemer, the Lord Jesus Christ. He saw our sad plight, alienated from God, poor, bankrupt, depraved and under sentence of death and hell, hopelessly and helplessly lost in sin. And He loved us so much that He purposed to redeem us and make us His own. Paul says "he loved us and gave himself for us." But to be our Redeemer, He must meet all the demands and the conditions of the law of God. This redemption must be in absolute justice and righteousness. If He fails to redeem us legally as well as voluntarily the redemption will not stand. See, therefore, how in the infinite wisdom of God, Jesus met all the conditions of our redemption. Remember the three basic requirements:

1. He must be related by birth and belong to the family of those to be redeemed.

2. He must be able to pay the price—he must be mighty and wealthy.

3. He must be willing to act as the redeemer.

The Bible sets forth how the Lord Jesus met all these conditions. First, the Redeemer must be a member of the family of fallen Adam. This is the first requirement of a kinsman-redeemer. But He was the Son of God—not the son of man. He was the Creator—not a creature. He belonged to the divine family—not the human family. As such He could not be the Redeemer. To be a Redeemer He must be a kinsman. He must enter the family of humanity, and right here we have the absolute indispensable necessity of the incarnation. So, in the omnipotence and omniscience of God, the Son of God became a man and came in the likeness of human flesh. The first step in this setting in motion the plan of redemption was the supernatural conception and virgin birth of the Saviour.

From a beginningless eternity Jesus was the infinite Son of God, one of the three persons of the trinity, equal with God the Father and the Holy Spirit. And then when the time for the payment of redemption's price came, Jesus left the glories of the Father's house, laid aside the form of God, stepped down from the parapets of heaven, and went down, down, down, down, past constellations and systems, through the measureless spaces of the heavens, through galaxies and innumerable groups of worlds, until He stopped at a comparatively infinitesimally small speck of matter we call this earth. He stopped at an insignificant village in Galilee, there to take up His abode in the womb of an obscure Jewish maiden, to be nourished by her blood, to grow like any other human in the dark recess of a mother's womb, to be born like any other baby, to cry, to smile, to creep, to walk, to suffer hunger and thirst, in weariness and pain, and finally pay the price of humanity's sin by dying like a criminal on a pagan cross. All this, to meet the first requirement of our redemption. The incarnation of the Son of God, the supernatural conception and the virgin birth of Jesus Christ is the bedrock of redemption. Without it all is lost — it is illegal — it is a violation of every principle of God's plan of salvation. To say that faith in the virgin birth of the Son of God is not essential to salvation is to reveal total ignorance of the Bible plan of redemption. Only a kinsman — a near relative was fit as a Redeemer.

Listen to Paul in Philippians 2, concerning Christ's condescension and incarnation. He says, speaking of Christ:

> Who, being in the form of God, thought it not robbery to be equal with God:

But made himself of no reputation, and took upon him the form of a servant, and was made in the likeness of men:

And being found in fashion as a man, he humbled himself, and became obedient unto death, even the death of the cross (Phil. 2:6-8).

Or listen to Galatians 4:

But when the fulness of the time was come, God sent forth his Son, made of a woman, made under the law,

To *redeem* them that were under the law, that we might receive the adoption of sons (Gal. 4:4, 5).

And the writer of Hebrews adds his testimony:

Forasmuch then as the children are partakers of flesh and blood, he also himself likewise took part of the same; that through death he might destroy him that had the power of death, that is, the devil;

And deliver [redeem] them who through fear of death were all their lifetime subject to bondage.

For verily he took not on him the nature of angels; but he took on him the seed of Abraham.

Wherefore *in all things* it behoved him to be made *like unto his brethren,* that he might be a merciful and faithful high priest in things pertaining to God, to make reconciliation for the sins of the people (Heb. 2:14-17).

THE KINSMAN-REDEEMER

This is our kinsman-redeemer. He is not ashamed to call them brethren. And just as Boaz stooped to be Ruth's redeemer at Bethlehem, so Christ was born in the city of the Redeemer. Make no mistake — faith in the virgin birth of Jesus Christ is a first requirement for salvation. Deny the virgin birth and incarnation of God in human flesh and you cannot be saved. You are still lost, no matter how religious.

Now we come to the second requirement of the law of redemption. The redeemer must be *able* to pay the price of redemption. We do not know how much Boaz had to pay to buy back Naomi and Ruth's lost inheritance or to pay up the back debts of his bride. But it must have been a large sum indeed. But Boaz was able, for the Holy Spirit has assured us that Boaz was a *mighty man,* and a *wealthy man.* Mighty and wealthy, and able to pay the price!

OUR MIGHTY REDEEMER

What a picture of the Lord Jesus this presents. For when He became poor for our sakes by becoming a man, He did not cease to be ALMIGHTY GOD. Jesus did not surrender His deity when He assumed humanity. He did not cease to be God when He became a man. Jesus was both ALMIGHTY GOD, and a man. As Almighty God, He commanded demons and angels, controlled the forces of nature, stilled the storms, multiplied bread, changed water into wine. As God He, like Boaz, had all authority. Boaz seems to have been the mightiest, most powerful and influential man in Bethlehem. I imagine he was the mayor. He sat down in the seat of absolute authority—the city gate. He commandeered his kinsman, and said, "Ho, such a one, sit down here" and the man asked no questions—he sat down. He commandeered ten elders and said, "Sit down here," *and they sat down.*

Our Redeemer is *all-*powerful, and Almighty. And He is wealthy enough to meet redemption's price. That price, about which we shall say more later, was the infinite price of life—a sinless life. The only remedy for death is life. To redeem us from death, He must give a life. Since life is in the blood, He must shed His blood for redemption. But it must be blood of infinite value. The blood of bulls and goats and sacrificial beasts could not atone for our sins. The blood of humanity could not atone, for it was polluted, sinful, corruptible, death-carrying blood. Even though a human being lived who had no sin, he could give his life for only one other sinner, because the blood of one person is limited to one individual. The Redeemer must, therefore, be able not to save just one, but be able to pay the price of redemption for a whole world of sinners.

This called for supernatural blood with infinite value. And this only Jesus provided. Because He was human, He could take man's place; because He was God, He could pay the infinite price by His infinitely effective, supernatural, divine blood. And so we see that our Redeemer met the first two conditions of a kinsman. He was related by birth — a human — yet supernatural birth, which made Him a member of the human family. But He must also be able to pay the infinite price, and so Jesus was also God — perfect God, omnipotent God, and like Boaz, *mighty* and *wealthy*.

Must Be Willing

One more requirement. There is a third condition. The kinsman must be willing. It must be voluntary. This condition too our Saviour met. Jesus did not have to redeem us. He chose to do so out of His love for us. We all deserve to go to hell, but only His love, His grace, provides the way. In Hebrews 10 we read:

> For it is not possible that the blood of bulls and of goats should take away sins.
>
> Wherefore when he cometh into the world, he saith, Sacrifice and offering thou wouldest not, but a body hast thou prepared me:
>
> In burnt-offerings and sacrifices for sin thou hast had no pleasure.
>
> Then said I, Lo, I come [in the volume of the book it is written of me,] to do thy will, O God (Heb. 10:4-7).

Yes, indeed, our great Kinsman-Redeemer was willing, willing to die, willing to give His life, that we might live.

> There was one who was willing to die in my stead,
> That a soul so unworthy might live.

And the path to the Cross He was willing to tread,
All the sins of my life to forgive.

Ah, my friend, are you willing to respond to that wonderful redemptive plan, and willingly receive Him as your personal Saviour now? God help you, and God bless you.

CHAPTER TWENTY

Born of a Woman

GOD'S plan of redemption was conceived in the mind of God from eternity. Before a speck of matter had been created, and God was all alone from a beginningless eternity, He foresaw and foreknew the fall of man and his need of a Redeemer. This plan whereby man would be "bought back," was settled before the worlds were made, and Jesus is called "the Lamb that was slain from before the foundation of the world." For four thousand years after man sinned, God prepared the world for the coming of the person of the Redeemer, who must, in order to meet God's requirements, be a member of the race whom He was to save. The actual carrying out of this plan of redemption begins with the Incarnation of the Son of God in human flesh.

> But when the fulness of the time was come, God sent forth his Son, made of a woman . . . (Gal. 4:4).

The Son was God Himself. He is called the Word of God.

> In the beginning was the Word, and the Word was with God, and the Word was God.
> The same was in the beginning with God (John 1:1, 2).

This eternal Son of God came down, and in some mysterious, inscrutable manner became a complete and perfect human being without surrendering His deity. John adds:

> And the Word was made flesh, and dwelt among us . . . (John 1:14).

To be a perfect human being He must have flesh and bone and blood. In His body He must BEAR our sins, but by His blood He must PAY for our sin. Just as Boaz was able to assume the burden of Naomi's and Ruth's debt and then pay the price of redemption, so Christ met the redemption price for us, and this price was His own blood.

Jesus lived on earth in this human body for a little over thirty-three years. At the beginning of this period of time stands His Incarnation, and at the end stands the Resurrection. The span of life Jesus lived on earth is bounded by the two greatest miracles in history—the Incarnation and the Resurrection. And between these two stands the Cross. There He shed His blood and made full satisfaction for our sins. The result of His Incarnation is His Resurrection as the proof that the penalty was paid. The Resurrection is the greatest evidence of the virgin birth of Jesus. The beginning and the end of His life are the unassailable evidence of His deity and omnipotence.

God was able to produce a sinless, perfect human being out of the flesh of a human race by a supernatural conception of the Holy Spirit, but as His life began with a demonstration of omnipotence, so His ministry closed with the same demonstration of almightiness, for the virgin birth and the Resurrection of Jesus Christ are inseparably united like the two pillars of one great arch. Take one away and the other crumbles. Deny the virgin birth and you have no explanation for His Resurrection. Take away His Resurrection literally and bodily, and the virgin birth loses all its meaning. If He must die like others and remain in death like others, there is no point in His exceptional birth. For this reason no matter what else a man may believe or reject concerning the Lord Jesus Christ, there can be no salvation without faith in the two fundamental facts of the Gospel: the deity of Jesus Christ and His bodily Resurrection.

All Because of the Blood

But the Resurrection of Christ is proof of another great fact. It is the final proof of the fact that while Jesus received His body from the Virgin Mary, His blood was a supernatural contribution—the blood of God Himself (Acts 20:28). Had Jesus' blood been human blood, it would have perished and completely corrupted during His three days and nights in the tomb. The blood of the sacrificial animals of the Old Testament was corruptible and decayed and was soon gone, but the blood shed on Calvary was imperishable blood. It is called incorruptible. Peter says:

> Forasmuch as ye know that ye were not redeemed with corruptible things, as silver and gold . . .
> But with the precious blood of Christ . . . (I Pet. 1:18, 19).

The blood of the Lord Jesus was sinless blood, and therefore incorruptible, for sin brought corruption, and where no sin is, there is no corruption. Every drop of blood which flowed in Jesus' body is still in existence just as fresh as it was when it flowed from His wounded brow and hands and feet and side. The blood that flowed from His unbroken skin in Gethsemane, the blood that was smeared about His back as the cruel, weighted thongs cut through His flesh as the flagellator scourged Him, the blood that oozed out under the thorny crown and flowed from His hands, His head, His feet, was never destroyed, for it was incorruptible blood. David speaks of Him in the sixteenth Psalm which Peter quotes in Acts 2, saying:

> Thou wilt not leave my soul in hell, neither wilt thou suffer thine Holy One to see corruption (Acts 2:27).

Although the body of the Lord Jesus Christ lay in the tomb in death for three days and three nights, no corruption had set in, for that body contained incorruptible blood. Lazarus being dead only one day more was said by his sister to be

STINKING with corruption, but this One saw no corruption because the only cause of corruption, SINFUL BLOOD, was absent from His flesh. That blood, every drop of it, is still in existence. Maybe when the Priest ascended into heaven, He went like the high priest of old in the Holy of Holies into the presence of God to sprinkle the blood upon the mercy-seat in heaven, of which the material mercy-seat and ark in the Tabernacle were merely copies. In Hebrews 9 we read:

> It was therefore necessary that the patterns of things in the heavens [referring to the earthly tabernacle] should be purified with these; [that is, the blood of beasts] but the heavenly things themselves with BETTER SACRIFICES THAN THESE.
> For Christ is not entered into the holy places made with hands, which are the figures of the true; but into heaven itself, now to appear in the presence of God for us:
> Nor yet that he should offer himself often, as the high priest entereth into the holy place every year with blood of others;
> . . . but now once in the end of the world hath he appeared to PUT AWAY SIN by the sacrifice of himself (Heb. 9:23-26).

After Christ had made the Atonement, He arose from the tomb, and then as the eternal High Priest, ascended into heaven to present the blood in the Holy of Holies where God dwells, and that blood is there today pleading for us and prevailing for us. The priest in the Tabernacle never spoke a word. All he did was PRESENT THE BLOOD and that was enough. Maybe there is a golden chalice in heaven where every drop of that precious blood is still in existence, just as pure, just as potent, just as fresh as two thousand years ago. The priest in the earthly Tabernacle needed to repeat the sprinkling again and again; and it is significant that among all the pieces of the furniture of the Tabernacle there was no chair to be found. We read of the altar, the table, the candlestick, and the ark, but you will find no chair in the

Tabernacle of Israel. It simply signified that the work of the earthly priest who sprinkled the blood of animal sacrifice was never done. He could not sit down. His work was never finished. But of the great High Priest, Jesus Christ, we read:

> But this man, after he had offered one sacrifice for sins for ever, SAT DOWN on the right hand of God . . .
> For by one offering he hath perfected FOR EVER them that are sanctified (Heb. 10:12, 14).

The blood has been shed—the incorruptible, eternal, divine, sinless, overcoming, precious blood! It availed then, and it avails now and throughout all eternity it shall never lose its power.

> Dear dying Lamb, Thy precious blood
> Shall never lose its power,
> Till all the ransomed Church of God
> Be saved to sin no more.

Because of all this, the blood is called in Scripture by many descriptive names. "It is precious," says Peter. "It is incorruptible," says David. "It is overcoming blood," says John in Revelation, for "they overcame him by the blood of the Lamb and by the word of their testimony." No wonder Satan hates the blood and will do anything to get rid of that power of the blood of Christ.

Today, it is as true as in the day of Israel, that there is no remission without the blood. When the men of Beth-shemesh looked upon the law of God without blood, they perished. Today, the law has not changed its character, nor the blood. The law still is the "ministration of death" (II Cor. 3:7). It is still true that, "Cursed is everyone that continueth not in all things which are written in the book of the law to do them." They that are of the works of the law are under the curse. "The letter (*law*) killeth" (II Cor. 3:6).

ONLY THE BLOOD

God said to Israel and to us, "When I see the blood I will pass over you." He did not say, "When I see your goodness, your morality, your works, your fervent religious worship, your earnestness in trying to keep the Ten Commandments or observe the Golden Rule." No, it is simply this: "When I see the blood I will pass over you." Do you think that I have made too much of the blood, and have overemphasized its importance? Listen! Blood is mentioned in the Bible about SEVEN HUNDRED TIMES from Genesis to Revelation, and when we see the redeemed throng in heaven in the Book of the Revelation, we hear them singing, not about their goodness, not about how they have kept the law and been faithful, but this is the song:

> Unto him that loved us, and washed us from our sins in his own blood (Rev. 1:5).

> Have you been to Jesus for the cleansing power?
> Are you washed in the blood of the Lamb?
> Are your garments spotless? Are they white as snow?
> Are you washed in the blood of the Lamb?

CHAPTER TWENTY-ONE

The Missing Bride

WEDDING bells are ringing in the little village of Bethlehem in Judea. A public wedding to which everyone was invited is being solemnized in a thoroughly impressive and legal way. It is an outdoor wedding, held in the public square at the gate of the city. The record is brief but inexhaustible in its precious lessons. We read the impressive story in Ruth 4:9-11,

> And Boaz said unto the elders, and unto all the people, Ye are witnesses this day. . . .
> Ruth the Moabitess . . . have I purchased to be my wife . . . ye are witnesses this day.
> And all the people that were in the gate, and the elders, said, We are witnesses (Ruth 4:9-11).

This is the brief account of the marriage of Boaz and Ruth. After Boaz had removed the last obstacle to his marriage, by eliminating the other near kinsman, he publicly speaks his vows, and the witnesses subscribe to the ceremony and say, "We are witnesses." This was the simple ceremony.

SOMETHING MISSING

But there is something strikingly strange about this wedding in the gate of Bethlehem. There is something missing, a fact which most Bible students have overlooked. Where is the bride? Ruth is strangely absent, and it is all done by the bridegroom, Boaz. Evidently the bride was sitting quietly at home, awaiting the coming of the groom to tell her the wedding was over and everything was completed. She does not appear at the ceremony at the gate, but the last we saw of her is in the closing verse of chapter three. Naomi had said unto her, after her return from the threshingfloor of Boaz:

> Sit still, my daughter, until thou know how the matter will fall: for the man will not be in rest, until he have finished the thing this day (Ruth 3:18).

And after that, it is all Boaz, all the way. Compared to weddings today this was certainly a strange procedure. Today the bride steals the whole show from beginning to end and the poor bridegroom is little more than an unimportant but necessary appendage. He is completely lost in a maze of activities, all designed to honor the bride. Whose picture appears on the society page when the engagement is announced? The bride, of course. The groom is only mentioned because—well, because if you are going to be married, there must be someone to marry. And for whom are all the showers planned? The bride, of course. Linen showers, china showers, personal showers, kitchen showers, but how often do you hear of a shower for the groom? And then the wedding. Again it's all the bride! The groom is scarcely noticed, as he meekly follows the preacher and takes his place of waiting patiently for the procession to climax in the appearance of the bride; as the organ booms out "Here Comes the Bride." Why don't they play "Here Comes the Bridegroom"? The father gives the bride away, but who gives the groom away? All eyes are on the bride, and when the reception line forms, why doesn't someone beside his weeping mother kiss the bridegroom as well as the bride?

And then when the account of the wedding appears in the paper, it is all about the bride, her veil, her jewels, her dress, her slippers, her bouquet — but what about her husband? Now all of this, of course, is humorous, and some of you may consider it frivolous, but we haven't said these things to be funny just for the sake of humor. We would not waste our valuable time in frivolity. I have overplayed this account for a very definite purpose, to show how strikingly different was the wedding of Boaz and Ruth. There Boaz the bridegroom is in the limelight and is the most important party in the union. Ruth is out of the picture. Her only claim to honor was that she became Mrs. Boaz.

OUR GREAT BRIDEGROOM

All this is in perfect harmony with the spiritual teaching of the whole Book of Ruth. It is the book of redemption of a poor, impoverished, penniless widow, who according to the law had no rights or claims to press. Everything must be done by another. According to the law, Ruth was an outcast. A Moabite was under the curse and estranged from the covenant nation of Israel. By law she was excluded from the congregation of God's people (Deut. 23:3).

In Nehemiah 13, after the children of Israel had returned from the Babylonian captivity this law was still in effect, and we read:

> On that day they read in the book of Moses in the audience of the people; and therein was found written, that the Ammonite and the Moabite should not come into the congregation of God for ever (Neh. 13:1).

The law barred the way for poor Ruth. She could do nothing about it but cast herself upon the mercy of her redeemer. And here grace stepped in and did that which the law was powerless to do. The law knows no mercy — only justice. And so Boaz acts in grace and accepts Ruth by paying the price the law demanded, and redemption is accomplished.

Jesus the Redeemer

Ruth represents the Church in general and the believer in particular. Boaz is the clearest type of Christ in the role of Redeemer anywhere in the Scriptures. By nature we are like Ruth under the curse and the judgment of God. We have no claim to His favor, but are aliens and strangers, shut out from the blessing of salvation. The law stands as the inflexible guardian of the righteousness and holiness of God, barring the way for the sinner. The law demands perfection, and perfect, uninterrupted, complete obedience to its every precept. There are no exceptions to the law of God. One single infraction of the law — one evil thought, one angry word, one dishonest act, one single lie, is a breach of the whole law.

> For whosoever shall keep the whole law, and yet offend in *one* point, is guilty of all (Jas. 2:10).

The law is a unit, and to break one single commandment is to break the entire law. And that broken law demands the punishment of death. If once during an entire lifetime a man should commit one wrong act — just one — he would be guilty and condemned before the law and worthy of death. The Bible leaves no doubt about this, and if any of you are ready to challenge that statement, I suggest you first read carefully what Paul says in Galatians 3:10:

> For as many as are of the works of the law are under the curse: for it is written, Cursed is every one that continueth not in ALL things which are written in the book of the law to do them.

Note well, there are no exceptions. Cursed is *every one*, and then notice, it must be *continuous* obedience. There must be no interruptions. And finally notice, it must be *continuous, unbroken obedience to the whole law*.

This then leaves us like Ruth without a single claim to the blessing of God. We are hopeless, helpless, lost and condemned. But there is hope for all such. Boaz by his love for Ruth acted in grace, paid her past account, and then, by marrying her, assumed all responsibility for any future debts she might incur. What a complete provision! He cleaned up her past debt and made himself responsible for all future obligations. This was grace.

In the very same way the Lord Jesus our Redeemer saw our sad plight, our hopeless, helpless condition under law, and in grace assumed responsibility for our great debt of sin and paid the infinite penalty of a broken law, providing for us the guarantee of all future provision. And so Paul, after telling us that the law condemns one and all, continues in Galatians 3:13:

> Christ hath *redeemed* us from the curse of the law, being made a curse for us: for it is written, Cursed is every one that hangeth on a tree (Gal. 3:13).

The law said "Stay out," but grace says "Come in," the price has been paid.

And in all this great transaction, Christ alone like Boaz is the actor. We are wholly passive as far as doing anything toward our salvation. It is only ours to accept. We cannot lift one finger of our own efforts or works, but must trust Him to do it all. In fact, it was all done for us 1900 years ago before we were even born. At Calvary Jesus paid for our redemption. How could we possibly have any part in it when we were not even there?

BACK TO BOAZ

This brings us back to Boaz and Ruth in Bethlehem. Boaz did it all. Ruth evidently was not even there. Boaz spake his vow, but there is no record that Ruth spake her "I do" and "I will." It was Boaz who said the "I do" and "I will" and "I take thee as my lawful wife." You see, it all depended on Boaz. What a picture of our union with Christ! There too He does it all. It depends on *His* faithfulness, not ours.

Yes, in our modern weddings the bride steals the show — but not so at the Wedding of the Lamb. There He will be the center of worship and adoration. We owe all and everything to *Him*. All the Bride possesses is *in Him* and because of *Him*. All her righteousness is *in Him*. All her worth is because *of Him*. And so unlike our modern weddings, the Bible gives Jesus the prominent place in its description of that great wedding day. We are told how the Bridegroom will be dressed. In Revelation 1, we read that He was:

> . . . clothed with a garment down to the foot, and girt about the paps with a golden girdle.
>
> His head and his hair were white like wool, as white as snow; and his eyes were as a flame of fire;
>
> And his feet like unto fine brass, as if they burned in a furnace; and his voice as the sound of many waters.
>
> And he had in his right hand seven stars: and out of his mouth went a sharp twoedged sword: and his countenance was as the sun shineth in his strength (Rev. 1:13-16).

That is God's description of the Bridegroom — not the Bride. And again in Revelation 19, we have still other details added:

> His eyes were as a flame of fire, and on his head were many crowns . . .
>
> . . . his name is called The Word of God (Rev. 19:12, 13).

This is the write-up of the gloriously arrayed Bridegroom as He comes with His Bride. But all we have written of the Bride is:

> Let us be glad and rejoice, and give honour to him: for the marriage of the Lamb is come, and his wife hath made herself ready.

> And to her was granted that she should be arrayed in fine linen, clean and white: for the fine linen is the righteousness of saints (Rev. 19:7, 8).

That is all the description of the Bride. It is called the wedding of the Lamb — *not the bride*. And even her wedding gown is the gift of her husband. Yes, then we shall confess that all we are, we are because of Him. It is *His* riches which are ours. It is *His* righteousness which is imputed to us. We shall claim nothing of self, but give praise only to Him. The Bride will not steal the show. Then we shall be able to fully and adequately obey the admonition of Paul in Colossians 1:

> Giving thanks to the Father, which hath made us meet to be partakers of the inheritance of the saints in light:
> Who hath delivered us from the power of darkness, and hath translated us into the kingdom of his dear Son:
> In whom [*in whom*] we have *redemption* through his blood, even the forgiveness of sins:
> For *by him* were all things created . . . all things were created by him, and for him:
> And he is before all things, and by him all things consist.
> And he is the head of the body, the church: who is the beginning, the firstborn from the dead; that in all things he might have the *preeminence* (Col. 1:12-14, 16-18).

Oh, praise His wonderful name! When we were lost, when the law demanded our death, He came, paid the price of our redemption and has promised to forever love, protect, provide and keep all those who put their trust in Him!

> In loving kindness Jesus came
> My soul in mercy to reclaim;
> And from the depths of sin and shame
> Through grace He lifted me.
> He called me long before I heard,
> Before my sinful heart was stirred,

But when I took Him at His word,
Redeemed He lifted me

From sinking sand He lifted me,
With tender hand He lifted me,
From shades of night to plains of light,
Oh, praise His name, He lifted me!

CHAPTER TWENTY-TWO

The Price of a Slave

And Boaz said unto the elders, and unto all the people, Ye are witnesses this day, that I have BOUGHT all that was Elimelech's, and all that was Chilion's and Mahlon's, of the hand of Naomi.

Moreover Ruth the Moabitess, the wife of Mahlon, have I PURCHASED to be my wife . . . ye are witnesses this day.

And all the people that were in the gate, and the elders, said, We are witnesses. (Ruth 4:9-11).

A PUBLIC sale was held in the market place at the gate of Bethlehem. The articles for sale were a piece of property and a poor slave girl. It was a public auction and the high bidder was a wealthy land owner named Boaz. He was the only one who could meet the conditions and furnish the capital for this momentous business transaction. A poor woman, Naomi, had lost title to her husband's estate which could only be redeemed by paying all the back debts and taxes and penalties. This was now up for sale. In addition to this piece of real estate, there was a servant girl, a widow who also had a claim to this property, by virtue of a former marriage, but her husband had died and she was left penniless and widowed. Her name was Ruth.

According to the law, lost property could be redeemed by a near relative, providing he was willing and able to meet the price. The widow too could be redeemed if a near relative were able and willing to take her as his wife. These two things — Naomi's property and Ruth's widowhood — were up for redemption. Among those who were willing, only one could be found who was able to do so. His name was Boaz, a man of great influence and wealth. He calls a public meeting, counts out the money, receives title to the estate, and immediately marries the servant girl, Ruth.

WHAT PRICE DID HE PAY?

The Bible does not state the exact amount Boaz was required to pay for the redemption, but we do know it must have been a great sum and that it had to be paid in "silver." Silver in the symbology of Scripture is the currency of redemption. Silver is symbolic of blood. When God passed through Egypt on the night of Israel's deliverance, all the first-born in Egypt died, but in the homes of the Israelites not a dog moved his tongue, for they were saved by the blood of the redemption lamb upon the lintel and the door posts. Now the Lord did not pass by Israel because they were better than the Egyptians, but only because of the blood of redemption. They deserved to die as well as the Egyptians, but the price of redemption had saved them. As a reminder and a memorial of this, it became a law in Israel that the first-born of every animal should be redeemed by being sacrificed to the Lord. In Exodus 13 we read:

> . . . whatsoever openeth the womb among the children of Israel, both of man and of beast: it is mine.
> That thou shalt set apart unto the LORD all that openeth the matrix, and every firstling that cometh of a beast which thou hast; the males shall be the LORD'S (Ex. 13:2, 12).

These first-born were to be sacrificed as a reminder to Israel that they too deserved death. Therefore, they were to put to death and sacrifice all the first-born of their flocks and herds. But now comes a problem. If this is to be carried out, all the first-born of Israel would have to die, and so God provided a redemption for these. In Exodus 13 we read again:

> . . . the LORD slew all the firstborn in the land of Egypt, both the firstborn of man, and the firstborn of beast; therefore I sacrifice to the LORD all that openeth the matrix, being males; but all the firstborn of MY CHILDREN I redeem (Ex. 13:15).

In order to spare these first-born of Israel, a redemption price was required. This redemption price was to be a personal tax to be paid in silver coin. This silver was required of every male child of Israel, which is made clear in Exodus 30:

> When thou takest the sum [census] of the children of Israel after their number, then shall they give every man a ransom for his soul unto the LORD. . . .
>
> This they shall give, every one that passeth among them that are numbered, half a shekel [of silver] after the shekel of the sanctuary; . . . an half shekel shall be the offering of the LORD.
>
> The rich shall not give more, and the poor shall not give less than half a shekel . . . to make an ATONEMENT for your souls (Ex. 30:12, 13, 15).

This silver money is called "atonement" money which was required of every single male Israelite. Failure to furnish the silver meant death and cutting off from the congregation of Israel. Silver then in Scripture is "atonement" money, and since atonement was only by blood, silver always speaks of blood. Unless this silver was paid, it meant judgment. Many years later, David was to be painfully reminded of this lesson, that there can be no numbering of the people without the atonement money being paid. In II Samuel 24 and I Chronicles 21 we have David's great sin. He commanded a census to be taken and the people numbered. But David failed to collect the half shekel of silver which the law required, and the result was a plague in Israel which left 70,000 dead. No one can be numbered among the people of God without being redeemed by the blood of atonement symbolized by silver.

THE PRICE OF BLOOD

Silver was the price of blood. For this reason the foundation of the Tabernacle in the wilderness was made of solid silver, collected as a "blood tax" from the children of Israel. We have the record in Exodus 38:

> And the silver of them that were numbered of the congregation was an hundred talents, and a thousand seven hundred and threescore and fifteen shekels, after the shekel of the sanctuary:
>
> And of the hundred talents of silver were cast the sockets of the sanctuary, and the sockets of the vail; an hundred sockets of the hundred talents, a talent for a socket (Ex. 38:25, 27).

The Tabernacle in Israel rested entirely upon a foundation of silver, called atonement money and collected from the children of Israel. Silver, therefore, becomes a symbol of the price of atonement and redemption. As there is no atonement and redemption without blood, this silver is symbolic of the price God demanded for our redemption, viz. blood. In type it pointed to the bloody sacrifices of the Old Testament, but all of it was in anticipation of the precious blood of Christ.

LIFE IS IN THE BLOOD

The purchase price of silver was the price of LIFE for the life is in the blood. In Leviticus 17:11 we read:

> For the life of the flesh is in the blood: and I have given it to you upon the altar to make an ATONEMENT for your souls: for it is the blood that maketh an atonement for the soul (Lev. 17:11).

Silver then is definitely, and beyond a question of doubt, atonement money. Atonement is made by the blood, and therefore, the silver in the Tabernacle speaks of blood, and the Tabernacle rested on this foundation of blood. This silver foundation becomes a symbol, a most beautiful symbol, of the precious blood of the Lord Jesus Christ, which was shed on Calvary's Cross, on which our whole redemption rests and is builded as the only foundation.

. . . without shedding of blood is no remission (Heb. 9:22).

Our redemption has been bought at a great price. It was the price of the blood of the Son of God, for this silver under the Tabernacle was merely a type of the blood of our Saviour. Paul tells us:

. . . ye are bought with a price (I Cor. 6:20).

Peter tells us:

. . . ye were not redeemed with corruptible things, as silver and gold . . .
But with the precious blood of Christ, as of a lamb without blemish and without spot (I Pet. 1:18, 19).

It is called PRECIOUS blood. It means that it is of tremendous and inestimable worth. It was precious because it was the blood of God, not the blood of a man. Now if that statement seems to be strange and bold, we would remind you that the Bible clearly teaches that it was the "blood of God" which was shed on Calvary. The blood of the Lord Jesus Christ was not derived from man, but it was divine blood, and the divine contribution, the blood of God. Jesus was virgin-born, without a human father. The blood in Christ was a divine contribution. Paul settles this beyond all dispute in Acts 20:28, where he says to the Ephesian elders:

> Take heed therefore unto yourselves, and to all the flock . . . to feed the church of God, which he hath purchased with his own blood (Acts 20:28).

Notice the words — "the church of GOD, which he (God) hath purchased with His own (God's) blood." Since it was the blood of Christ, He must of necessity have been God, because it is called "the blood of God." Jesus is God, and His blood, therefore, was the blood of Almighty God Himself. No wonder that Peter calls it "precious blood."

Everything, therefore, depends upon the blood of Christ because it is divine blood. There is no salvation apart from personal appropriation of that blood by faith. Man may make light of it, and may refuse to accept it, but the fact remains, without the shedding of blood there is no remission, and without the blood of the Lord Jesus Christ there is absolutely no salvation. The natural man, of course, rejects this, and calls our theology a theology of the shambles and the butcher shop, but the fact remains that without this blood there is no approach to God. It is the very foundation, the very rock, the very silver foundation upon which all of our hope is built. If any man build on this foundation, he shall be saved.

> For other foundation can no man lay than that is laid, which is Jesus Christ (I Cor. 3:11).

BOAZ THE REDEEMER

Returning now to the book of Ruth and the price Boaz was required to pay for the redemption of Naomi's inheritance and the purchase of Ruth, we may be reasonably sure it was a large sum and that it was paid in silver. And what a picture it becomes of the price of our redemption, for nothing less than the blood of the Son of God was sufficient to pay the debt we owed, and to set us free. As a striking example of the meaning of silver as pointing to blood, we take you to the story of the betrayer of Jesus who sold his Master for thirty pieces of silver. Matthew records the story briefly as follows:

> Then one of the twelve, called Judas Iscariot, went unto the chief priests,
> And said unto them, What will ye give me, and I will deliver him unto you? And they convenanted with him for thirty pieces of silver (Matt. 26:14, 15).

This was the price of blood, and Judas soon found it out. After Satan had driven him to this dastardly betrayal, he cast Judas aside, and realizing how he had been deceived, he committed suicide.

> Then Judas, which had betrayed him, when he saw he was condemned, repented himself, and brought again the thirty pieces of silver to the chief priests and elders,
> Saying, I have sinned in that I have betrayed the INNOCENT BLOOD (Matt. 27:3, 4).

He does not say, I have betrayed an innocent person, but innocent *blood*. And now notice the testimony of the chief priests. They

> . . . took the silver pieces, and said, It is not lawful for to put them into the treasury, because it is the price of *blood*.
> And they took counsel, and bought with them the potter's field, to bury strangers in.
> Wherefore that field was called, The field of *blood*, unto this day.
> Then was fulfilled that which was spoken by Jeremy the prophet, saying, And they took the thirty pieces of silver, the price of him that was valued, whom they of the children of Israel did value;
> And gave them for the potter's field, as the Lord appointed me (Matt. 27:6-10).

Then after being sold for thirty pieces of silver, the price of a slave, the Lamb of God went to fulfill these types and shadows of silver by shedding His literal blood in Gethsemane, in the judgment hall, and on the Cross. There He fulfilled all the prophecies and types of His redemptive work, and now we can sing:

> Nor silver nor gold hath obtained my redemption,
> No riches of earth could have saved my poor soul;
> The blood of the Cross is my only foundation,
> The death of my Saviour now maketh me whole.

> I am redeemed, but not with silver;
> I am bought, but not with gold;
> Bought with a price — The blood of Jesus,
> Precious price of love untold.

CHAPTER TWENTY-THREE

From Poverty to Riches

And Boaz said unto the elders, and unto all the people, Ye are witnesses this day, that I have bought all that was Elimelech's, and all that was Chilion's and Mahlon's, of the hand of Naomi.

Moreover Ruth the Moabitess . . . have I purchased to be my wife (Ruth 4:9, 10).

WHAT a strange wedding at the gate of Bethlehem, for it is more than a wedding. It is a legal business transaction, whereby certain legal matters had to be settled before the marriage could be consummated. This involved the redemption of the lost property of the family of Elimelech. Boaz, by assuming the responsibility of paying up the past debts of the family of Ruth's first husband, removed the last obstacle. What price Boaz paid for this redemption we are not told, and for a very good reason, for Boaz was a type of the Lord Jesus, who paid the incalculable, infinite price of redemption in His own blood. The value of this blood cannot be reckoned, and so even in the type, the purchase price which Boaz was required to pay is not mentioned.

Two Purchases

But notice that two things were purchased by Boaz — a lost inheritance and a lost relationship. Boaz says: "Ye are witnesses this day that I have bought all" (Ruth 4:9), the forfeited property and possessions of the family of Naomi. Man by creation in the image of God was made a king over God's creation. He had dominion over all the earth (Gen. 1:26, 28). But man lost this inheritance through sin, and became a bankrupt slave to corruption and death, and his dominion over the earth was lost. Our Lord Jesus paid the price of redeeming this lost inheritance and when He comes to consummate our full redemption at His second coming, all creation will again be restored to its original perfection.

RUTH ALSO

But Boaz purchased something else. He purchased a wife. He says:

> Moreover Ruth the Moabitess, the wife of Mahlon, have I purchased to be my wife (Ruth 4:10).

She had to be "bought," for she was hopelessly in debt. By this act of redemption and the payment of the debts of Ruth by her relationship to Naomi, Ruth became the wife of Boaz. And thus the marriage was legalized, for every condition had been met. The witnesses endorse the transaction, and

> All the people that were in the gate, and the elders, said, We are witnesses (Ruth 4:11).

And then the wedding ceremony was appropriately closed with a prayer meeting, for the witnesses utter a wonderful prayer for the happy bride. Here is the prayer:

> The Lord make the woman that is come into thine house like Rachel and like Leah, which two did build the house of Israel: and do thou worthily in Ephratah, and be famous in Bethlehem:
> And let thy house be like the house of Pharez, whom Tamar bare unto Judah, of the seed which the Lord shall give thee of this woman (Ruth 4:11, 12).

Two remarkable, striking statements occur in this prayer which must not be overlooked. They are:

1. Be famous in Bethlehem.
2. Be like the house of Pharez.

The elders pray that Ruth might be famous in Bethlehem. We know now how that prayer was answered, for Ruth's great grandson was to be born in Bethlehem as the shepherd king David and great type of the coming Heavenly King Jesus who Himself was to be born in the same place some 1300 years later. It was indeed a prophetic prayer.

The second striking phrase in this closing wedding prayer is the reference to Pharez. They pray:

> And let thy house be like unto the house of Pharez . . . (Ruth 4:12a).

We shall have more to say about Pharez in our next message, but just here we mention that Pharez was a bastard, the illegitimate son of Judah, the son of Jacob. It is a demonstration of the grace of God by including in the ancestors of the Redeemer this unworthy object of God's wonderful mercy.

The Price of Redemption

Up until now we have not been occupied with the price of the redemption as given in the Scriptures. Redemption always involved the payment of the legal amount of money. This amount was fixed by law and was an inviolable obligation. Israel was to be constantly reminded of the price of their own redemption. They were to be reminded that they were once under the sentence of death in Egypt, but that by the blood of the Passover Lamb, they had been redeemed. That they might never forget this glorious redemption whereby their first-born were spared, the Lord claimed all the first-born of man and beast as His own by virtue of a redemption. The first-born of clean animals were to be given as a sacrifice to God. The first-born of unclean animals were to be redeemed with a lamb or else put to death by breaking its neck (Ex. 13:13). The first-born of the children of Israel were also to be redeemed. God had said:

> Sanctify unto me all the firstborn, whatsoever openeth the womb among the children of Israel, both of man and of beast: it is mine (Ex. 13:2).
> And it shall be when thy son asketh thee in time to come, saying, What is this? that thou shalt say unto him, By strength of hand the Lord brought us out from Egypt, from the house of bondage:
> And it came to pass . . . that the LORD slew all the first-born in the land of Egypt . . . therefore I sacrifice to the LORD all that openeth the matrix, being males; but all the firstborn of my children I REDEEM. (Ex. 13:14, 15).

ALL DESERVED TO DIE

It was God's way of telling them that they deserved to die, but had been redeemed by grace. The Israelites were no better than the Egyptians. They were not spared because they were any better than their oppressors, but because of the mercy and grace of God. It was all in the blood of the Passover Lamb. God had provided the redemption price and they were saved.

Like the Israelites and like Ruth the Moabitess, we too had no claim on God's mercy and grace. Unworthy, lost, hopeless and condemned by the law, our only hope was in another who was willing and able to pay the price of our redemption. By the intervention of Boaz, Ruth, a stranger and an outcast, was redeemed from her slavery and widowhood and inducted into the family of God's people all because of the love of another. We had nothing to bring, nothing to offer, but could only plead His marvelous grace.

By our birth like Ruth we were estranged from God. Paul tells us in Ephesians that we:

> . . . were dead in trespasses and sins:
> Wherein time past ye walked according to the course of

this world, according to the prince of the power of the air, the spirit that now worketh in the children of disobedience:

Among whom also we all had our conversation in times past in the lusts of our flesh, fulfilling the desires of the flesh and of the mind; and were by nature the children of wrath, even as others (Eph. 2:1-3).

Wherefore remember, that ye being in time past Gentiles in the flesh, who are called Uncircumcision by that which is called the Circumcision in the flesh made by hands;

That at that time ye were without Christ, being aliens from the commonwealth of Israel, and strangers from the covenants of promise, having no hope, and without God in the world (Eph. 2:11, 12).

This was our condition by our first birth. Ruth was a Gentile, under the curse, without hope in herself. By the love of Boaz she was taken into the family of the people of God, and so we continue in Ephesians 2:

But now in Christ Jesus ye who sometimes were far off are made nigh by the blood of Christ (Eph. 2:13).

Now therefore ye are no more strangers and foreigners, but fellowcitizens with the saints, and of the household of God (Eph. 2:19).

We who were outcasts and strangers become members of the first family of heaven. Ruth the bride of Boaz became partaker and heir of everything Boaz possessed. Words fail us entirely to describe the marvelous change for Ruth, the poor gleaner.

FROM POVERTY TO RICHES

This redemption was full and complete. First all of the past obligations and debts of the bankrupt family were paid in full. Boaz said, "Ye are witnesses that I have redeemed *all* that was Elimelech's." The whole past account was settled and closed. But that was not all. When Boaz took Ruth to be his wife, he also assumed the responsibility for any and all debts Ruth might contract in the future. As the wife of the wealthy, mighty Boaz, she became the possessor of all the wealth of her husband. Everything which Boaz had now belonged to Ruth. They held everything in "joint ownership." When a man and woman marry, they become one and they hold everything in common. The old liturgy for the confirmation of marriage contained the phrase spoken by the groom, "and with all my worldly goods I do thee now endow."

What a marvelous picture of our salvation by grace. Everything we have is because of *him*. All we are is because of *Him*. All we shall ever possess is because of *Him*. Our past debts are all paid. We are delivered because all our sins are under the blood, forgiven, erased, blotted out, forgotten and buried and put away. And all because of Him who:

> . . . hath made us meet to be partakers of the inheritance of the saints in light:
> Who hath delivered us from the power of darkness, and hath translated us in the kingdom of his dear Son:
> In whom we have redemption through his blood, even the forgiveness of sins (Col. 1:12-14).

For All Time

But the Lord has not only forgiven our past sins, but made provision for all our sins past, present and future. When Christ died to save us on the Cross, He knew how prone we would be to stumble and fall, even after we were saved, and so he made provision whereby we can come at any time to receive forgiveness and cleansing. He knew how far short *we* would come even after we were born again, and so he provided for the sins of the saints. He says:

> If *we* confess our sins, he is faithful and just to forgive us our sins, and to cleanse us from all unrighteousness (I John 1:9).

This was written to born-again believers and John includes himself in the "we." And again we read:

> My little children, these things write I unto you, that ye sin not (I John 2:1a).

The Christian should not sin, but the sad thing is that he all too often does sin. And our Lord knew this and so adds:

> And [but] if any man sin [those who ought not to sin], we have an advocate with the Father, Jesus Christ the righteous (I John 2:1b).

Yes, beloved, there is provision made for the past, the present and the future. If you have once known the joy of sins forgiven, but have slipped and fallen, do not despair and imagine you are lost, but come to Him, who today is your forgiving High Priest, ever living to make intercession for you. Come to Him, repent, confess and be restored again.

And to you who never knew Christ, come now before it is too late. No matter what your sin burden may be, Jesus offers to forgive, for He has paid the purchase price. If you will only come, He will not turn you away.

CHAPTER TWENTY-FOUR

Thy Will Be Done

THIS will be a very, very dry sermon for many of you. The genealogies of the Bible hold little interest for most people, but before you conclude them dull and uninteresting, I want you to consider one of the strangest genealogies, occurring in the strangest place. So don't lose interest, and you will be richly rewarded. The record is found in the closing portion of Ruth:

> So Boaz took Ruth, and she was his wife: and when he went in unto her, the LORD gave her conception, and she bare a son.
>
> And the women said unto Naomi, Blessed be the LORD, which hath not left thee this day without a kinsman, that his name may be famous in Israel.
>
> And he shall be unto thee a restorer of thy life, and a nourisher of thine old age: for thy daughter in law, which loveth thee, which is better to thee than seven sons, hath born him.
>
> And Naomi took the child, and laid it in her bosom, and became nurse unto it.
>
> And the women her neighbours gave it a name, saying, There is a son born to Naomi; and they called his name Obed: he is the father of Jesse, the father of David (Ruth 4:13-17).

Thus does the touching story of Ruth come to its happy ending. It began with tragedy, sorrow and disappointment. It begins with a famine in Bethlehem, deaths and burials in the land of Moab. It ends with wedding bells in Bethlehem and rejoicing at the birth of a precious baby. The story ends

176

with a happy grandmother, Naomi, nursing Ruth's baby and the women of Bethlehem giving its name.

Here the story should have ended, but instead there is added a genealogy. This was probably added under inspiration at a later date, or it may be that the Book of Ruth (whose author is not mentioned) was written many years after its occurrence. Whatever the case may be, the Holy Spirit added the closing five verses for a very definite purpose.

> Now these are the generations of Pharez: Pharez begat Hezron,
> And Hezron begat Ram, and Ram begat Amminadab.
> And Amminadab begat Nahshon, and Nahshon begat Salmon,
> And Salmon begat Boaz, and Boaz begat Obed,
> And Obed begat Jesse, and Jesse begat David (Ruth 4:18-22).

Strange ending indeed for a love story! Just a fragmentary genealogy, a single branch from a family tree! There are just ten names in this list, beginning with Pharez, son of Judah, and ending with David, king of Israel. It begins with a "bastard," and ends with a great king. It is the story of Grace, Grace, Grace, the story of a poor, unworthy Gentile widow becoming the happy bride of the wealthy Boaz. But the brief genealogy is for an additional reason, to show the righteousness and justice of God.

An Illegitimate Son

To illustrate the justice of God, David was the first man in Israel who had a right to Israel's throne. He was a descendant of Pharez, the illegitimate son of Judah. We have the sordid record in Genesis 38.

Judah the son of Jacob had married a Canaanitish woman who had borne him three sons, Er, Onan and Shelah. When Er was of age his father gave him a wife by the name of

Tamar. But Er died before he had an issue and died childless. According to the law of redemption of a wife, the brother of the deceased was to take his brother's wife. This the second son of Judah did, but he too died childless and left Tamar a widow again. There was one more son of Judah, Shelah, who was eligible to take the widowed Tamar. But Judah refused to give him to Tamar. It was then that Tamar the widow disguised herself as a harlot and enticed Judah, her own father-in-law, to become the father of her child. This baby was called Pharez. He was an illegitimate child, born of Judah and his own daughter-in-law.

God's Law Stands

Now the Bible had given very clear instructions concerning the place of such an one in Israel. The significance of all this will become evident as we see God's provision. It begins, therefore, with Pharez, and then there follow nine names, making a total of ten — just ten. No more. No less. Just ten: Pharez, Hezron, Ram, Amminadab, Nahshon, Salmon, Boaz, Obed, Jesse, and David. Exactly ten in number! Jesse, the father of David, the king, was the ninth, and David himself was the tenth.

Believing as we do in the verbal and infallible inspiration of the Scriptures we immediately look for a reason for this strange ending in the Book of Ruth. We have the answer given, however, when we turn to Deuteronomy 23, verse 2. Here is God's own commandment in regard to a situation of this very kind.

> A bastard shall not enter into the congregation of the Lord; even to his tenth generation shall he not enter into the congregation of the Lord.

Here is the definite command of the Lord that no child born out of wedlock should ever be admitted into Israel until the tenth generation. Nine, as we told you, is the number of judgment, and the judgment of sin must first be fulfilled. Only after nine generations may a person, therefore, who is a descendant born of this unholy practice, take his place in testimony, for ten is the number of testimony.

GOD'S WORD ALWAYS HOLDS

The expression, "a bastard shall not enter the congregation," had reference to a place in the royal line of Israel. It did not imply being a social outcast. Ancient rabbis interpreted it to mean that no descendant of a bastard could sit upon the throne of Israel until the tenth generation. This seems to be the correct meaning as recorded in the actual history of Israel.

God never departs from His Word, and generations afterward He keeps His command. It was, therefore, impossible for any of the descendants of Pharez to sit on Israel's throne for ten generations, and when Israel under Samuel demanded a king, God could not give them a legitimate king from the royal tribe of Judah, because the curse of Deuteronomy 23:2 still rested upon them. When Israel demanded a king, it was only the ninth generation since Pharez, the son of sin, the son of Judah. Jesse who was then in the line was only the ninth. David was the tenth, but was not yet ready, probably not yet born. Since the curse of ten generations was upon the line of Judah, the kingly line, until David should be ready for the work of the Lord, God could not honor the request of Israel for a king and so He steps outside the tribe of Judah into the tribe of Benjamin, and gives them Saul, the son of Kish, instead. This was their choice — never God's choice, only to be rejected by the Lord Himself as soon as David, the tenth, was ready in the purpose and program of God.

DIVINE INSPIRATION

In the light of all this, can you deny or doubt the supernatural, infallible inspiration of the Scriptures? If I personally had no other evidence of the supernatural authorship of this wonderful Book than this closing genealogy in Ruth, it would be entirely enough for me.

Ruth then was written to prove the legal genealogy of God's coming king of Israel, David the great redeemer. Ruth was David's grandmother and one of the five women mentioned in the genealogy of Jesus Christ, the royal Son of David, as given in the first chapter of the Book of Matthew.

We would make a very practical application right here. Less than two hundred years after the story of Ruth occurred, Israel was to learn the great lesson that God's Word cannot be broken. He had said:

> A bastard shall not enter into the congregation of the LORD; even to his tenth generation (Deut. 23:2).

In I Samuel 8, Israel demands a king to reign over them. They said to Samuel:

> Now make us a king to judge us like all the nations.
> But the thing displeased Samuel when they said, Give us a king to judge us. And Samuel prayed unto the LORD (I Sam. 8:5, 6).

Now there was nothing wrong in Israel's desiring a king. God had promised them a king, but it must be God's man and not Israel's choice. But it was not God's time, for the first one eligible to be king was David, the tenth one in the line of Pharez, who was under the curse. When Israel demanded a king, God's man David was not yet ready. He was probably not even born, but if he was, he was too young to assume the kingship. Jesse the father of David was only the ninth in the line of Pharez and so ineligible. But Israel could not wait God's time and so demanded a king. Listen to God's answer to Samuel's prayer:

> And the Lord said unto Samuel, Hearken unto the voice of the people in all that they say unto thee: for they have not rejected thee, but they have rejected me, that I should reign over them (I Sam. 8:7).

And then Samuel proceeds to tell them of the disaster which Saul, their own chosen king, would bring upon them in impoverishing and oppressing them (I Sam. 8:9-17), and lead them down into dismal defeat upon Mount Gilboa. And then we have God's warning:

> And ye shall cry out in that day because of your king which *ye shall have chosen you;* and the Lord will not hear you in that day.
> Nevertheless the people refused to obey the voice of Samuel; and they said, Nay; but *we will* have a king over us (I Sam. 8:18, 19).

The story of King Saul is one of the saddest in the history of Israel. God could not give them a king from the royal tribe of Judah because David was the tenth in the line. And so as soon as David, God's choice, was old enough, the Lord rejects Saul, he dies a miserable suicide, and God sets up *His* king, and ushers in the golden reign of David when Israel reached its greatest heights of power.

Not My Will, But Thine

What is the lesson in all this? We are to submit our will to His. How prone we (like Israel) are to demand things of God which are not His will for our lives. Instead of submitting to Him and making God's will more important than our own desires, we demand that God answer our prayers according to our desires.

Are you in trouble today and seek for relief? Remember

God has a purpose in leading you in this way. If you could see what God is doing, you would understand, but God wants us to walk by faith. Are you suffering and ill and desire to be healed? There is nothing wrong in asking God to heal you, but it must always be, "If it be Thy will." Maybe God's will is otherwise for a reason we shall some day know. Do your prayers seem to go unanswered? Then remember God may have a reason for the delay. He knows what He permits is best for us. If we were to receive our wishes, it might prove to be a greater tragedy. When people write to us asking prayer for healing, for relief from trouble and for special blessing, we always pray first of all that He may give grace to accept God's answer, whatever it may be. To be in the will of God is most important. It is better to suffer in the will of God than to have our own way and miss the will of God.

Many years ago I was called to visit a heartbroken mother who told me the following sad and tragic story. Never did I behold greater grief. This mother said to me, "For several years after our marriage we had no children. We besought the Lord to give us a child, and He answered with a baby girl. When the child was two years old, she contracted pneumonia and we were told by the doctors there was no hope. In agony and despair I rebelled against God, and said, 'Oh, God, you can't do this to us. You can't be so cruel as to take this child away. I cannot—I will not give her up. You must restore her or I'll lose all faith and will never trust Thee again.' Well, the child recovered miraculously, and grew to be a young lady, but got into bad company, sank deep into sin, and one night was picked up by the police in a dark alley, and taken to jail for an unspeakable act. The next morning as the jailor came to her cell, he found her strangled by a rope made of her torn clothing—a suicide."

I shall never forget the agony of that mother. Said she, "Oh, doctor, if I had only buried her when an infant, when I demanded my own way. Her death then would have been a thousand times easier than this. Oh, God forgive me, forgive me for my willful, selfish demand." God granted her request, but what a hard way to learn to pray "not my will, but Thine be done"!

I close with a verse to illustrate the point. In Psalm 106:15 David recounts Israel's experience in the wilderness. They were dissatisfied with God's provision of the manna and desired meat. God gave it to them, but it proved to be poison for them, and they died like flies in their gluttony. Recalling this experience David says:

> He [God] gave them their request; but sent leanness into their soul.

Oh, to learn the lesson of trust and faith, and be able to say with our great Example, Jesus, "Not my will but Thine," even though it means Calvary. But Calvary leads to the resurrection and victory.

> Wherefore let them that suffer *according to the will of God* commit the keeping of their souls to him in well doing, as unto a faithful Creator (I Peter 4:19).